MW00784834

EVERY STAMP

EDITED BY CHERYL R. GANZ WITH M. T. SHEAHAN

THE NATIONAL PHILATELIC COLLECTION

FOREWORD BY RICHARD R. JOHN

TELLS A STORY

A SMITHSONIAN CONTRIBUTION TO KNOWLEDGE

Smithsonian Institution
Scholarly Press

WASHINGTON, D.C.

2014

Published by
SMITHSONIAN INSTITUTION SCHOLARLY PRESS
P.O. Box 37012, MRC 957
Washington, D.C. 20013-7012
www.scholarlypress.si.edu

Copyright © 2014 by Smithsonian Institution

All rights reserved. No part of this publication may be reproduced, stored in a retrieval system, or transmitted in any form or by any means, electronic, mechanical, photocopying, recording, or otherwise, without the prior permission of the publisher.

All images are courtesy of the Smithsonian National Postal Museum unless otherwise noted. Images are not to scale.

Cover images: Front cover inspired by the 2¢ Warren G. Harding stamp of 1923; spine includes the 24¢ Inverted Jenny stamp of 1918; and the back cover features the 29¢ Smithsonian National Postal Museum imperforate block of four (cropped).

Library of Congress Cataloging-in-Publication Data:
Every stamp tells a story : the National Philatelic Collection / edited by Cheryl R. Ganz, with M.T. Sheahan ; with a foreword by Richard R. John.
 pages cm. — (A Smithsonian contribution to knowledge)
   Includes index.
   ISBN 978-1-935623-42-7 (hardcover : alk. paper) — ISBN 978-1-935623-54-0 (ebook) 1. National Postal Museum (U.S.) 2. Stamp collections—United States. 3. Postage stamps—History. 4. Postage stamps—United States—History. 5. Postal service—United States—History. I. Ganz, Cheryl. II. Sheahan, M. T.
   HE6204.U5E94 2014
   769.56074'753—dc23

2014014611

ISBN-13 (print):   978-1-935623-42-7
ISBN-13 (ebook):   978-1-935623-54-0

Printed in the United States of America

∞ The paper used in this publication meets the minimum requirements of the American National Standard for Permanence of Paper for Printed Library Materials Z39.48–1992.

To the Smithsonian Institution curators and stewards who have cared for
the National Philatelic Collection and made it accessible to visitors on-site and online
and to William H. Gross for making a new home for this national treasure a reality.

CONTENTS

FOREWORD

The postage stamp is an icon of modernity. Few artifacts better symbolize the far-flung webs of communications that since the mid-nineteenth century have transformed the world. Far more than the electric telegraph—and, until quite recently, to an extent as great as the telephone and the Internet—the mail has fostered sociability by dissolving the age-old barriers that divided families and friends who lived apart. The mail has also been an indispensable instrument of commerce and, in many countries, including the United States, a cornerstone of the infrastructure for the circulation of information on public affairs.

It is thus a cause for celebration that the Smithsonian National Postal Museum has remounted its renowned collection of postage stamps and mail in a grand, historic, and appropriate setting—the former main post office in Washington, D.C. Thanks to the munificence of philanthropist William H. Gross, the public will henceforth have the opportunity to view thousands of postal objects that have until now been hidden away in a vault. The centerpiece of the William H. Gross Stamp Gallery is the National Philatelic Collection—the greatest collection of U.S. postage stamps and related production specimens in existence, as well as one of the largest and most comprehensive collections of postage stamps and postal markings from the rest of the world.

Every Stamp Tells a Story provides an engaging introduction to the National Philatelic Collection, with a focus on the United States. Its contributors, each an authority on his or her topic, have brought a wealth of knowledge to the challenging task of locating individual postage stamps in their political, cultural, and economic setting, without losing sight of the fascination that these artifacts hold for the many hobbyists who call themselves philatelists. The postage stamps of the United States are truly "Windows into America," as curator Cheryl R. Ganz aptly observes in one of her essays for this volume. Their content offers a fast-moving panorama of evolving patriotic ideals and persons (consider the ever-expanding array of people and themes that stamp designers have commemorated over the years) while their form reflects the remarkable technological transformations that have shaped their production, distribution, and usage.

The word philatelist is a nineteenth-century neologism that combines two Greek words—*philo* and *ateleia*—which can be roughly translated as "a lover of something that is exempt from taxation." The word reminds us that postage stamps are receipts for a transaction that has yet to occur, making them fitting emblems of a relationship that is founded ultimately on trust. This volume provides philatelists and nonphilatelists alike with fresh insights not only into postage stamps as artifacts but also into the future-oriented cultural moment that gave rise to their invention and that remains a hallmark of the global communications network today.

Richard R. John
Professor
Columbia Journalism School

PREFACE AND ACKNOWLEDGMENTS

Images on stamps have influenced the course of history and honored people and places around the world. They have drawn attention to social issues and raised money for important causes. Stamps also provide clues to their production and usage, recording important changes in design, technology, and communications. Every stamp and piece of mail tells a story. In fact, most tell multiple stories.

The National Philatelic Collection is the largest continuously intact museum collection in the world. It is the second largest collection, after that of the National Museum of Natural History, of the Smithsonian Institution. The bulk of the collection is philatelic, objects related to postage stamps in all production stages and usage, and the focus of this book. Amazingly, until now, a book has never been published about this collection of over six million treasures, many unique.

I once told my friends that my dream job was to be a curator at the Smithsonian Institution, and we would all laugh at such a seemingly lofty and impossible goal. But then, in America, it is amazing how often dreams do come true. As chief curator of philately, I lead a team of talented staff to oversee the philatelic curatorial duties of the National Philatelic Collection. I have been richly rewarded not only by viewing and researching great rarities and great collections but by creating compelling exhibits on-site and online to reach millions of visitors and connect to their interests.

So many fascinating people enjoy lives that revolve around the world of stamps and mail, including the Council of Philatelists, a museum advisory board. I thank all those who have given support and nuggets of information. They have helped me maintain the continuity of knowledge for the curators and keepers of the collection as it moves through its second century of educating and surprising scholars with discoveries.

The idea for a book about the National Philatelic Collection flowed from my role as lead curator for the new philatelic exhibition space, the William H. Gross Stamp Gallery. Preparation spanned over seven years. This world's largest stamp gallery opened 22 September 2013. Conceptualizing the seven gallery spaces within the stamp gallery forced me to think about the National Philatelic Collection as a whole, not just segments of its wonderful holdings. This national treasure deserved a new home and a new tome.

I am grateful to my predecessor and mentor, W. Wilson Hulme II. I have also benefited greatly from a dedicated and knowledgeable staff in the Department of Philately, including Curator Daniel A. Piazza; Assistant Curators Ken Gilbart, Marvin Murray, and Michael Plett; Guest Curators Richard Bates, Ronald Lesher, and David Straight; Research Associates Richard Bates and Herbert Trenchard; and Museum Specialists Katie Burke and Michael Devaney. M. T. "Terry" Sheahan has written and edited scripts and text for on-site and online. I have also worked with script writers Sharon Barry and Esther Ferington. Their words have influenced me and this book.

The Smithsonian National Postal Museum staff is experienced and masterful. Every single person has been essential to creating a new standard for postal museums worldwide, and all contribute to the safety and care of the National Philatelic Collection. It was my honor as lead curator to chair the content team for the William H. Gross Stamp Gallery. I am especially grateful to noncuratorial colleagues on that team and the stamp gallery exhibition team leadership, including Allen Kane, director; Amy Borntrager, development; Pat Burke, exhibits; Marshall Emery, public relations; Linda Edquist, conservation; Glen Hopkins, design and construction management; Elizabeth Schorr, collections; Roxanne Symko Smith, project management; and K. Allison Wickens, education. In addition, I thank Polone Bazile, finance; Nancy A. Pope, history of postal operations; Kim Wayman, finance; and the many dozens of staff, contractors, and volunteers who contribute to everyday success. I regret that I cannot name every one of you.

I thank my fellow curators who wrote chapters: Richard Bates, Lynn Heidelbaugh, Ronald E. Lesher, Nancy A. Pope, and Daniel A. Piazza. In addition, Dan Piazza and Thomas Lera contributed information for chapters. Caitlin Badowski, Michael Devaney, Kellyn Hoffman, Thomas Lera, Bill Lommel, James O'Donnell, Annette Shumway, Ted Wilson, Design and Production Incorporated, and Gallagher & Associates assisted with images. I am grateful to proofreaders Alan Warren and Robert Odenweller, both top philatelic scholars. Colleagues and reviewers at Smithsonian Institution Scholarly Press offered

excellent guidance. I could not have accomplished this volume while simultane-
ously working as lead curator on the William H. Gross Stamp Gallery without
M. T. Sheahan's exceptional wordsmithery and shared vision for the book.

Cheryl R. Ganz
Curator of Philately Emerita
Smithsonian National Postal Museum

1

THE WORLD OF STAMPS AND THE INVERTED JENNY
Cheryl R. Ganz

In 1840, in response to demand created by its steady industrial and commercial expansion, England issued its first postage stamp, the Penny Black. Postal reformer Rowland Hill argued that the existing system, in which the receiver paid the postage based on distance, no longer served the public well. He suggested an alternative—the sender prepay the postage based on its weight. The change ignited a communications revolution that transformed the world by making mail more affordable and reliable for commerce and individuals (Figures 1 and 2). The images on postage stamps provided a simple means of education. To this day, images emblazoned on these tiny bits of paper proclaim national culture, sentiments, and history.

Sometimes a stamp becomes very famous for reasons other than, for instance, its origin, use, or image. Occasionally, a stamp or sheet becomes famous because something goes amiss during the printing process, producing an error. Philatelists love errors because they occur so infrequently and the search for an error is so much fun.

The most famous error in U.S. philatelic history—the "Inverted Jenny"—occurred in May 1918 with the printing of the nation's first airmail stamp (Figures 3 and 4). The bicolor 24¢ stamp features a blue image of the JN-4-H Curtiss Jenny, the plane selected to initiate official airmail service with its flight between Washington, D.C., and New York City. A red frame borders the vignette. Printers used the spider press to produce the issue. The process required two runs through the press, one for the frame and one for the plane. After finishing one impression, the printer removed the plates, reinked them, returned them to the press for the next impression, and reinserted the paper. This process resulted in considerable variation among stamps and, in this case, a fabulous blunder—an upside-down airplane. No one today knows for sure how the Inverted Jenny error occurred. During the second pass, an employee either reversed the plate with the central design or reversed the sheet with the frame. Only one sheet of errors slipped past printing inspectors and into the marketplace (Figures 5–7).

The invert in and of itself is spectacular, but there have been other inverts. What makes this one so famous? Its particular uniqueness lies in its follow-up story. Stamp collectors eagerly awaited the nation's first airmail stamps. Aware that the two-pass process could produce inverts, an avid collector, William T. Robey, rushed to a Washington, D.C., post office early on 15 May, the first day of issue. Spotting a sheet of 100 with inverted images, Robey immediately purchased it. As it turned out, Robey's was that one and only sheet that had escaped the Bureau of Engraving and Printing's production department (Figures 8 and 9). From the moment the sheet passed into private hands, it claimed a life of its own. It has been sold, divided, and sold again. Examples have been stolen and faked, and one stamp was swept into a vacuum. More recently, it has been the object of a highly publicized trade. So the Inverted Jenny's fame lies not only with its inverted vignette; its mystique lies in its century of travels. Of all the Smithsonian National Postal Museum's gems, it is the most celebrated and the most frequently requested.

FIGURE 1

On 1 May 1840, Great Britain issued the world's first postage stamp, the Penny Black. It features the profile of young Queen Victoria, the reigning British monarch in 1840, and revolutionized postal services worldwide.

FIGURE 2

Rowland Hill (1795–1879) published a pamphlet titled *Post Office Reform: Its Importance and Practicability* in 1837. In this document, Hill recommended that postal fees be prepaid with "a bit of paper . . . covered at the back with a glutinous wash." The British government incorporated Hill's idea in the British postal reforms of 1839.

FIGURE 3
The 24¢ Curtiss Jenny stamp of 1918 with the inverted blue plane in a red frame is one of the world's most famous printing errors. Only one sheet of 100 escaped into the market.

FIGURE 4

The Curtiss JN-4-H, "Jenny," a World War I airplane reconfigured to carry mail, made the first regular airplane mail service flight, from Washington, D.C., to Philadelphia to New York. The first airmail stamp bears its image, including its number.

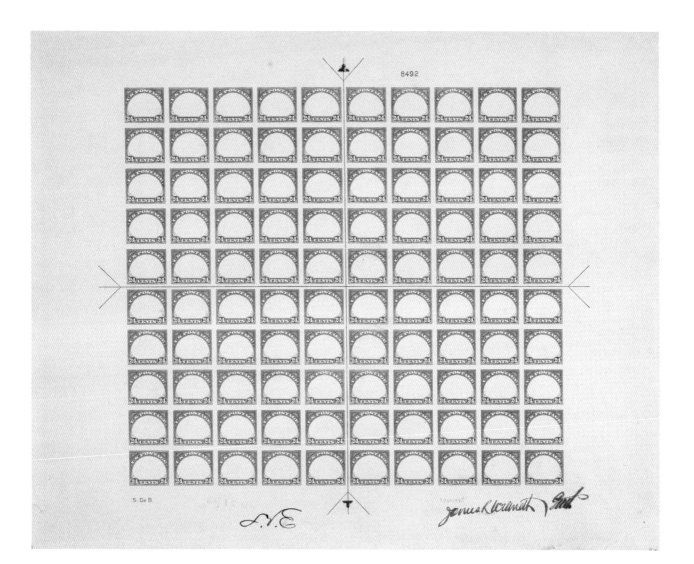

FIGURE 5
On 10 May 1918, a printer inked the plate, placed a sheet of paper on top, and fed the paper into a spider press to print the red frames of the Jenny airmail stamp.

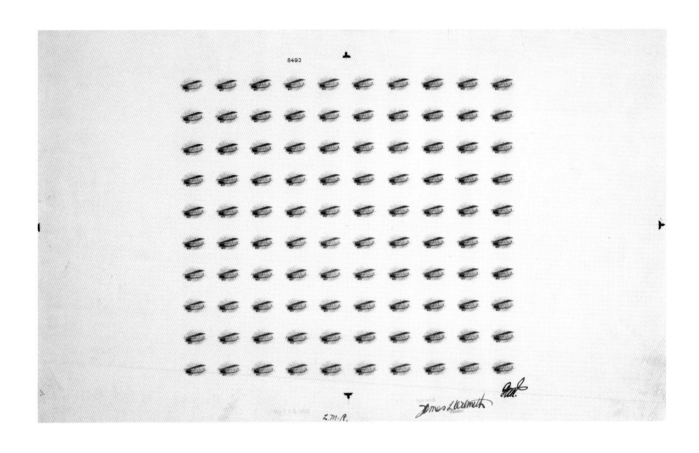

FIGURE 6
On 11 May, the blue airplanes were printed.

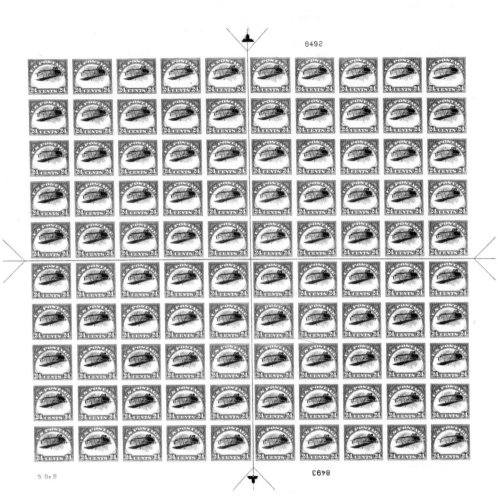

FIGURE 7
The result was a sheet of Inverted Jenny
stamps similar to this recreated sheet.

FIGURE 8
William T. Robey bought the one sheet of 100 airmail stamps with the invert. He described his discovery as "a thrill that comes once in a lifetime."

FIGURE 9
William T. Robey bought the sheet of 100 inverts at the New York Avenue post office, Washington, D.C., on the first day of sale.

2

GEMS OF AMERICAN PHILATELY
Cheryl R. Ganz

Philatelic gems, like gems of the mineral world, tell very special stories. They are frequently rare, they are highly prized, and they often chronicle great historical events. Most collectors only dream of owning such a treasure. The National Philatelic Collection includes many U.S. philatelic gems in addition to the Inverted Jenny. Each recounts a milestone in modern history and sheds added light on a familiar event, from the American Revolution to the landing on the Moon.

In 1765, Parliament passed *An Act for Granting and Applying Certain Stamp Duties in the British Colonies and Plantations in America*, commonly called the Stamp Act. Resisting the act was the first incremental step on the road to the American Revolution. Mounting cries of taxation without representation and public violence against the stamp agents eventually led Parliament to repeal the act on 18 March 1766 (Figures 10 and 11).

After declaring independence from Great Britain, Americans pushed beyond the colonies, creating a demand for simpler and more reliable means of communication. The Post Office responded with numerous improvements, including prepaid postage stamps. The National Philatelic Collection includes the original models for the nation's first two postage stamps, issued in 1847. The essay vignettes of Benjamin Franklin and George Washington were printed from existing engravings by Asher B. Durand. The frames were drawn in pencil and ink on cardboard, then a light wash of India ink was brushed on to give tone. When the first federal postage stamps were issued, the United States comprised twenty-nine states along with several territories. The Franklin stamp paid the rate for each half ounce sent up to 300 miles. The Washington stamp paid the rate for longer distances or heavier mail (Figures 12–14).

Collectors have always sought the fragile Hawaiian Missionary stamps, the first issued by the Kingdom of Hawaii in 1851. They are known as such because of their use by Christian missionaries in Hawaii. Their charming design and fancy numerals, along with Hawaii's exotic location, also make them highly desirable. The stamps are unusual because they paid various rates, including postage for a letter from Hawaii to the U.S. East Coast via San Francisco (Figures 15–18).

During the nineteenth century, letters traveled by coach, boat, ship, train, and the much-glamorized Pony Express. The Pony Express existed for such a brief period, April 1860 to October 1861, that surviving letters are unquestionably gems. On one ride, Indians overtook a Pony Express rider carrying mail from San Francisco, interrupting delivery and probably killing the rider. The mochila, or saddle bag, was later recovered. Two letters survived, one in superb condition because it had been wrapped in oiled silk cloth for protection. It bears an oval marking that reads "The Central Overland California & Pikes Peak Express Company," which then administered the Pony Express. Forwarded to its destination, it reached New York in 1862. By then, the Pony Express no longer existed (Figure 19).

Only one cover has ever been postmarked on the Moon (Figures 20 and 21). During the 1971 Apollo 15 mission, astronauts David R. Scott and James Irwin spent three days exploring the Moon from the Lunar Roving Vehicle. On the last day, Scott reached under the rover's seat for a pouch. It held an envelope bearing die proofs of two space stamps. Scott postmarked this cover while, 238,000 miles away, the U.S. Postal Service issued the stamps on Earth. The first postmark Scott made was faint, so he made another below it. The smudges on the left side are "thumbprints" made by his space suit glove.

Not all stamps in the National Philatelic Collection are gems such as these, but each tells a story of the American experience.

FIGURE 10
The 1-penny Stamp Act of 1765 revenue
stamp proof is one of the thirty-two
surviving red proofs of the Stamp Act
controversy.

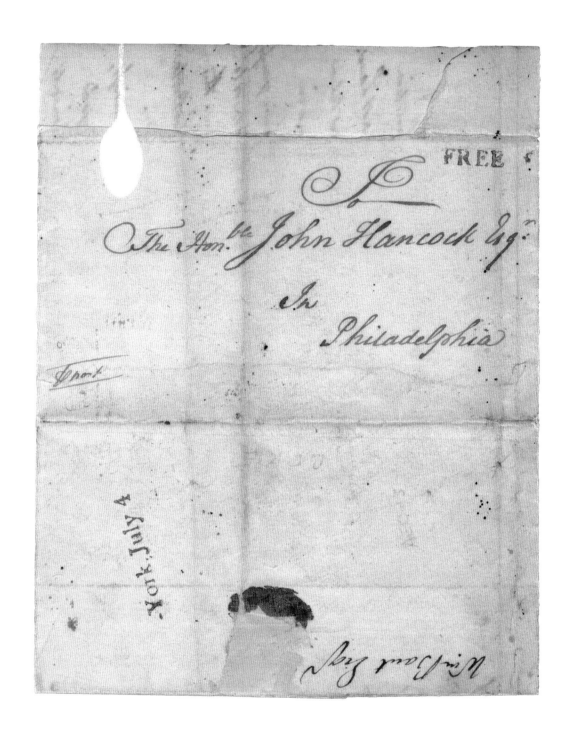

FIGURE 11

Marked "[New] York July 4," this letter was sent to founding father John Hancock by his lawyer on the day the Declaration of Independence was ratified in 1776.

FIGURE 12
The 5¢ Benjamin Franklin original model is one of the essays, or trial designs, created for review by postal authorities for the first U.S. postage stamps of 1847.

FIGURE 13
The 10¢ George Washington model of 1847 features a portrait of the first president of the United States. Washington and Franklin have been depicted on more U.S. postage stamps than any other Americans.

FIGURE 14
This 10¢ George Washington pair on cover is the earliest known use of a U.S. postage stamp. The stamps became valid for use on 1 July 1847, and the stamps here were used the next day. Courtesy of William H. Gross.

FIGURE 15

The first four stamps of the Kingdom of Hawaii became known as "Hawaiian Missionaries" because most were used on correspondence mailed by Christian missionaries. This 2¢ single was printed in 1851.

FIGURE 16

Henry Whitney, Hawaii's first postmaster, designed and printed the kingdom's first stamps, including this 5¢ single, on the press used to print the government newspaper.

FIGURE 17

Hawaii's first 13¢ stamp, issued in 1851, prepaid rates in the Kingdom of Hawaii and the United States. It read, "Hawaiian Postage."

FIGURE 18

Because the 13¢ stamp issued in 1851 confused postmasters in the United States, a redesigned 13¢ stamp appeared in 1852. It read, "H. I. & U. S. Postage."

FIGURE 19
This Pony Express cover, bearing a 10¢
Washington stamp, is one of the most
historically significant in the United States.
A notation reads, "Recovered from a mail
stolen by the Indians in 1860." Courtesy of
William H. Gross.

FIGURE 20

As part of the Apollo 15 lunar mission, on 2 August 1971, U.S. astronaut David R. Scott postmarked this first-day cover on the moon, an act as nationally significant as planting the flag. Courtesy of the United States Postal Service, Postmaster General's Collection.

FIGURE 21

Astronaut David R. Scott took this photo of James Irwin, the lunar module *Falcon*, and the Lunar Roving Vehicle. Courtesy of NASA.

3

HISTORY OF THE NATIONAL PHILATELIC COLLECTION
Daniel A. Piazza

The history of the National Philatelic Collection tells a story of changing attitudes, needs, and aspirations. Early curators of the Smithsonian's U.S. National Museum did not consider philately—the collection and study of postage stamps and mail—a discipline in its own right. Instead, they collected and exhibited stamps as historical curiosities. In 1886, the Smithsonian acquired a pane of engraved 10¢ blue Jefferson Davis stamps issued by the Confederate States of America in 1863 and displayed it alongside uniforms and battle flags as a trophy of the Civil War (Figure 22). Most subsequent acquisitions, including a rare proof of the 1765 Stamp Act revenue stamp, were exhibited as strictly historical artifacts with no reference to their philatelic importance.

When the National Museum's fine art and scientific exhibits moved from the Arts and Industries Building to the building that today houses the National Museum of Natural History, the vacated northwest court of the Arts and Industries Building was set aside for the stamp collections. In October 1913, the Smithsonian hired Joseph Britton Leavy, a retired brewery executive known in New York philatelic circles, to prepare the first permanent stamp exhibit. His job title was "government philatelist," and the exhibit, which opened in December 1914, marked the first time that the Smithsonian displayed stamps as philatelic specimens (Figure 23).

Catherine Manning succeeded Joseph Leavy, who died in 1921, and she retired in 1951. She curated the Smithsonian's philatelic collection for thirty years, longer than anyone else in its history. Under Manning's leadership, the philatelic collection became the largest in the National Museum's Division of History. Philately became a department in its own right in 1943. At the same time, the title "government philatelist" was retired when Manning was promoted to assistant curator, becoming the first woman to achieve curatorial rank in the Smithsonian outside of the sciences.

Franklin Bruns became the Smithsonian's philatelic curator after Catherine Manning retired. His six years as curator witnessed the collection's remarkable growth. A former newspaperman with a flair for turning a phrase, Bruns articulated his vision for a "National Philatelic Collection" and was the first to use that term regularly.

For the most part, Leavy and Manning had acquired material passively, depending on donations from individuals and periodic transfers of material from the Post Office Department. Bruns, on the other hand, aggressively solicited the philatelic holdings of other government agencies. He and his successors negotiated transfers of philatelic material from the Library of Congress, Government Printing Office, Bureau of Engraving and Printing, and Treasury Department and successfully cultivated private donors and acquired highly specialized research collections of foreign material, postal history specimens, and topical collections.

After nearly forty years on the third floor of the National Museum of American History (as the National Museum of History and Technology was renamed in 1980), the National Philatelic Collection was relocated to a home of its own in a museum dedicated to the history of postal operations and philately. The Smithsonian National Postal Museum opened in Washington's former City Post Office on 30 July 1993. Ten thousand people visited on opening weekend and stood in line for up to an hour to buy the four stamps issued for the occasion (Figure 24).

In recent decades, the Smithsonian's philatelic curators have worked to refine the National Philatelic Collection from a high of thirteen million stamps down to the current six million. This was achieved primarily through the sale of seven million duplicate, obsolete revenue stamps that had been transferred from the U.S. Treasury Department beginning in 1954.

Today, curators carefully consider each new acquisition, confirming that it meets the needs of the twenty-first century. They no longer aspire to complete the worldwide collection. Curators have sought philatelic objects from other institutions for acquisition, such as the Harry L. Jefferys collection. Long-term loans complement the National Philatelic Collection, including the Benjamin K. Miller and United States Postal Service (USPS) Postmaster General collections. From completing the stamps of the Kingdom of Hawaii, the Confederate States of America, and the Canadian provinces to acquiring stamp albums of famous personalities such as John Lennon and Ansel Adams to adding original sketches from USPS artists and art directors, curators seek individual pieces to tell powerful stories that capture the imagination of philatelists and noncollectors alike (Figure 25).

FIGURE 22

This 10¢ Jefferson Davis Type II sheet of 1863 was the first philatelic item acquired by the Smithsonian Institution, gifted by M. W. Robertson in 1886.

FIGURE 23

Visitors peruse the Smithsonian's stamp collection on display in the northwest court of the Arts and Industries Building, circa 1914.

It is adjacent to Union Station on
Capitol Hill in Washington, DC.

FIGURE 24

Block of four of the 29¢ Smithsonian
National Postal Museum commemorative
stamps from one of the two sheets (out of
7.5 million sheets printed) that escaped
from the American Bank Note Company's
plant without being perforated in 1993.

FIGURE 25

Smithsonian curators of philately, 1913 to present. (a) Joseph Britton Leavy, 1913–1921; (b) Catherine Lemmon Manning, 1922–1951, courtesy Library of Congress; (c) Franklin Richard Bruns Jr., 1951–1957 and 1972–1979; (d) Francis J. McCall, 1957–1963; (e) George Townsend Turner, 1958–1963; (f) Carl H. Scheele, 1959–1963 and 1971–1977; (g) Reidar Norby, 1966–1988; (h) James H. Bruns, 1984–1997; (i) W. Wilson Hulme II, 2002–2007; (j) Cheryl R. Ganz, 2005–2014; (k) Daniel A. Piazza, 2008 to present.

4

CREATION OF THE NATIONAL STAMP COLLECTION
Cheryl R. Ganz

The National Philatelic Collection contains nearly six million postage stamps, pieces of mail, and related ephemera from all over the world. Out of this vast and unique holding—unequivocally the finest of its kind in the nation—a committee of Smithsonian curators and other leading experts selected nearly 4,000 U.S. items to be placed on permanent exhibit as the "National Stamp Collection." Setting criteria for the selection, making choices, cataloging selections, organizing into an exhibit framework, researching and writing a narrative and captions, designing panels to hold objects, and preparing objects for exhibition took seven years of collaboration. The last time a large-scale representative display of U.S. stamps had been attempted by a curator was a century ago. A new century required a new vision. Curator W. Wilson Hulme II engaged a committee drawn from the museum's Council of Philatelists to select stamps and related philatelic objects for display. Harry "Sonny" Hagendorf, James Kloetzel, W. Curtis Livingston, Charles Shreve, Charles Verge, and Alan Whitman traveled to Washington, D.C., several times a year to search for special items in the vault. The process included surveying the museum holdings and developing a comprehensive collection of single stamps—one of each stamp issued through World War II—grouped in order of issue with essays, proofs, multiples, covers, and collateral material. At the same time, the committee identified key missing items (Figures 26 and 27).

The team methodically searched the shelves and drawers and boxes to find the hidden treasures. The first cut included anything that might be used. After the staff added objects to the museum database system, the committee began culling with digital images. The committee worked with Elizabeth Schorr,

Caitlin Badowski, and other collections department staff and later with Curator Cheryl R. Ganz, whom Hulme assigned in 2006 to lead the project. The committee rated each selection according to rarity, appeal, and condition. The National Stamp Collection strategy stressed completeness and uniqueness. The team created a list of missing items, and curators purchased some of them to fill gaps.

When Curators Ganz and Daniel A. Piazza received the final list of approximately 5,000 selected items, they began to conceptualize a historical framework with sections for display. The stamps fit into the first 100 years of postage stamps, 1847 to 1946. The curators developed time-era groupings in which historical events, post office history, and stamp issues fit together. After moving the selections into these eras, curators decided to add prestamp and post–World War II sections at the beginning and end to total ten chapters. In addition, curators followed Secretary G. Wayne Clough's "grand challenge" to the Smithsonian units to make "our artifacts and specimens tell wonderful stories illustrating the great American spirit" as part of a paninstitutional focus on the theme of American identity and diversity. Curators removed duplicate objects and added more covers, filled historical gaps, and sought balance to the story. The final number of objects for display totaled nearly 4,000 (Figures 28–31).

Then the behind-the-scenes work began. Assistant Curators Marvin Murray, Kenneth Gilbart, and Michael Plett worked with Ganz, Schorr, and Badowski to refine data and selections. Ganz and Piazza worked with writer M. T. Sheahan, Museum Education Chair K. Allison Wickens, the exhibition content team, and other staff to develop and proof an object list and script with narrative, titles, and captions. Designers at Gallagher and Associates created layouts for 350 panels, each individually designed and printed. In the meantime, the conservation and preservation department prepared objects for mounting on the panels so that they would be ready in time to install for the opening of the William H. Gross Stamp Gallery. All in all, this major task that created a monumental work will last well into the twenty-first century.

FIGURE 26
W. Wilson Hulme II (standing), chief curator of philately from 2002 until his death
in 2007, selects pieces for the National Stamp Collection with Council of Philatelists
members Charles Shreve (center) and Curtis Livingston (right).

FIGURE 27
Council of Philatelists member Alan Whitman reviews the National Stamp Collection
selections in the museum database with Accessions Officer Caitlin Badowski.

FIGURE 28
Preservation Specialist Manda Kowalczyk
examines each object to determine its
condition and need for further stabilization
before mounting for long-term exhibition.

FIGURE 29

Conservator Helen Young removes glue from the back of a rare stamp. Expert conservation treatments ensure longer, safer life spans for stamps and mail.

FIGURE 30

Conservator Linda Edquist mounts stamps, housed in protective clear polyester film, onto panels for the National Stamp Collection pullout frames in the William H. Gross Stamp Gallery.

FIGURE 31

Curators of Philately Cheryl R. Ganz and
Daniel A. Piazza with the National Stamp
Collection panels on display in new pullout
frames.

5

THE NATIONAL STAMP COLLECTION
Cheryl R. Ganz, Daniel A. Piazza, and M. T. Sheahan

The National Stamp Collection, consisting of nearly 4,000 items selected by experts for their representativeness, belongs to every American and is held in trust by the museum. The carefully crafted collection, a permanent cornerstone exhibit of the William H. Gross Stamp Gallery, tells the history of the United States in a new way—a story told by the images on stamps, stamp production, postage rates, and markings on mail. For display purposes, curators divided the collection into ten historically based eras, with stamps and mail matter chronicling those periods, beginning before the American Revolution. Professor Richard R. John of Columbia University, the country's leading academic historian of communication technologies, has described the collection as illuminating the nation's political, cultural, and economic history. Further, he says it provides "visitors with an authoritative, nuanced, and engaging contextualization of these remarkable artifacts" (Figure 32).

Before colonists declared independence in 1776, England provided a postal service that facilitated transatlantic exchanges rather than intercolonial communication (Figure 33). Within decades of the revolution, a postal system united the former colonies. To serve constituents, congressional representatives' mail went free of postage, and the cost of mailing newspapers was low. High rates for letters limited other correspondence. Those *receiving* the correspondence generally paid the postage, which a postmaster at the sending office had handwritten or stamped on the envelope. Private carriers delivered the mail and collected the fee.

Western expansion and the Civil War created other demands, prompting changes within the Post Office Department, which streamlined service by extending the web of postal roads, lowering postal rates, and, in 1847, introducing the first prepaid U.S. postage stamps. The stamps honored the nation's first postmaster and first president—Benjamin Franklin and George Washington. On 31 May 1861, after the South's secession, the Union suspended postal service to the Confederate States of America and soon issued new stamps. The Confederacy issued a stamp of its own in October. Confederate stamps featured images of great Southern leaders (Figure 34). Even though citizens swore allegiance to one side or the other, their letters often crossed lines into enemy territory. The patriotic cachets and markings on Civil War mail tell stories ranging from friendship to adversity.

Postwar industrial progress allowed the Post Office to experiment with new machinery, and much lower rates ignited a communications revolution that provided the backdrop for other changes, including the necessity to better serve the business sector. Rural Free Delivery, Parcel Post, and the standardization of universal postal rates undergirded the industrial boom, giving people worldwide access to the nation's manufactured products. To accommodate commerce, new formats such as coils and booklets appeared. A period of prosperity saw the popularization of leisure activities such as stamp collecting. In 1893, the first commemoratives stamps appeared to celebrate the 400th anniversary of Columbus's discovery of the New World (Figures 35 and 36). The next year, the Post Office Department granted an exclusive contract to print stamps to the Bureau of Engraving and Printing.

During the twentieth century, the rise of corporate America, wars, the economic depression, technology, and cultural transformation all affected the Post Office Department and the stamps issued (Figure 37). Corporate communications, catalog sales, and direct marketing demanded a response from the Post Office, which made changes in its products and services. The rush of immigrants from southeast Europe and Russia prompted the issuance of stamps with images of American power and progress, a form of history lesson. During the Great Depression and Franklin D. Roosevelt's early presidential administrations, redesigned, streamlined stamps suggested hope and national endurance (Figures 38 and 39). Airmail, formally introduced in 1918, filled a crucial need during World War II, connecting loved ones on the battleground and home front (Figure 40). Stamps bore designs with patriotic themes, and designs reflected the influence of politicians.

The cultural and technological changes following the Vietnam War and continuing into the twenty-first century are profoundly evident in postal services and the subject matter depicted on postage stamps. Although at one time only the images of famous Americans—presidents, scientists, and educators—appeared on stamps, now stamps produced by commercial printers rather than the Bureau of Engraving and Printing reflect America's more diverse population and colorful popular culture.

a

b

c

d

FIGURE 32

The National Stamp Collection Index and Stamp Icons. (a) 1750–1847, Early America, 10¢ St. Louis Bear Type 1 postmaster provisional, 1845; (b) 1847–1861, Reform and Expansion, 3¢ George Washington, 1851; (c) 1861–1866, Civil War Era, 15¢ Abraham Lincoln, 1866; (d) 1867–1893, Industrial Revolution, 3¢ Steam Locomotive G Grill, 1869; (e) 1894–1908, American Century, 5¢ John Fremont on the Rocky Mountains die proof; (f) 1908–1916, Rise of Corporate America, 1¢ Benjamin Franklin, 1908; (g) 1917–1932, Boom and Bust, 2¢ Warren G. Harding imperforate, 1923; (h) 1933–1940, New Deal, 5¢ National Parks Yellowstone, 1934; (i) 1940–1947, World War II, 3¢ Win the War, 1942; (j) 1948 to present, Modern America, $1 Rush Lamp and Candle Holder invert error, 1979.

e

f

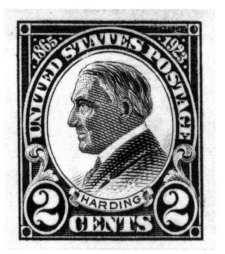

g

h

i

j

FIGURE 33

Benjamin Franklin, as deputy postmaster general under Britain's Parliamentary Post, enjoyed free franking privileges—that is, free postage. He signed this 1766 cover "B Free Franklin."

FIGURE 34

(a–c) This copper printing plate consisting of 400 subjects bearing the image of Confederate President Jefferson Davis in 5¢ denomination survived as a spoils of war. In 1862, the American federal warship *Mercedita* drew alongside the British steamer *Bermuda*, a blockade-runner. The boarding party found this plate and a consignment of some five million stamps printed for the Confederacy by Thomas De La Rue & Co, Ltd, London. The collection has a complete set of Confederate stamps.

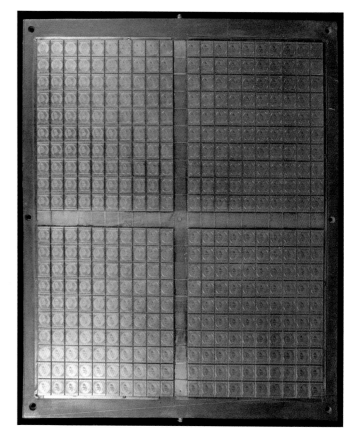

a

b

c

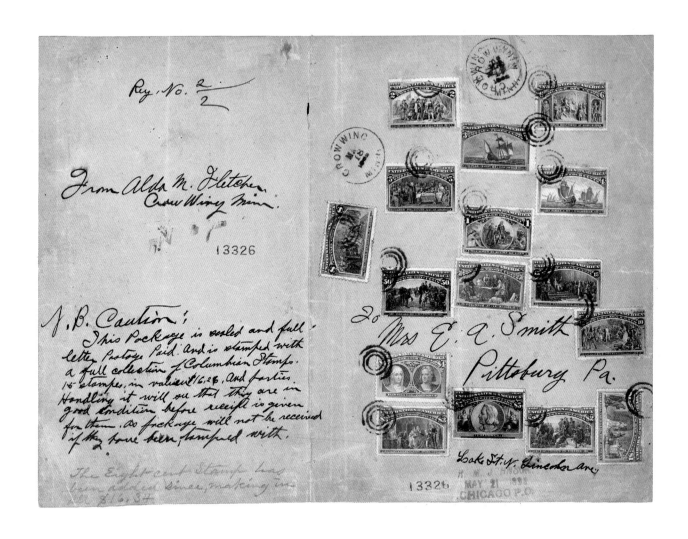

FIGURE 35

The Post Office Department issued its first commemorative stamps in 1893. This wrapper bears a complete set of the sixteen stamps illustrating the story of Columbus and issued in conjunction with the World's Columbian Exposition, held in Chicago, Illinois.

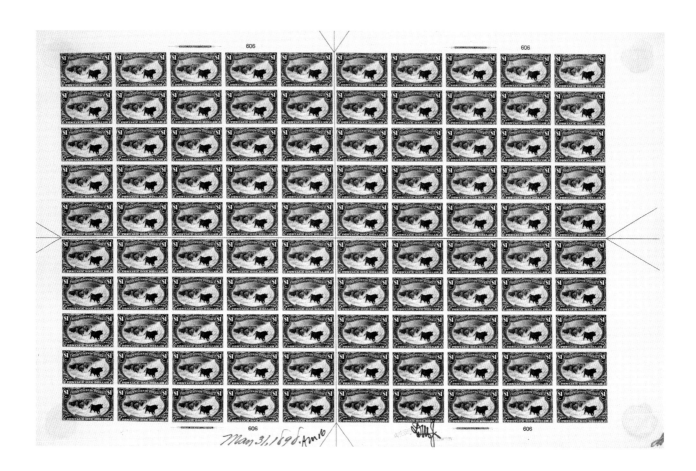

FIGURE 36

Certified plate proofs are the last printed proof of the plate before printing the stamps. Many philatelists consider this $1 Trans-Mississippi Western Cattle in Storm, printed in 1898, to be America's most exquisitely engraved stamp.

In 1930, the Post Office Department issued three stamps depicting Germany's LZ-127 *Graf Zeppelin* to subsidize its Pan American flight to South America, North America, and back to Germany. The Washington, D.C., post office postmarked this envelope on 19 April, the first day of issue of the three stamps before the cover flew on the entire round trip.

FIGURE 38

When President Franklin D. Roosevelt, an avid stamp collector, saw the model for the 3¢ Susan B. Anthony stamp of 1936, based on a marble bust by sculptor Adelaide Johnson, he sketched a revision and added a dark oval frame around the portrait of the women's rights activist.

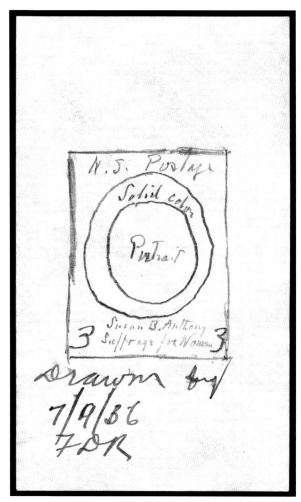

FIGURE 39

The die proof shows the dramatic result of his cameo idea.

FIGURE 40
Mailed by a U.S. sailor, this cover was postmarked 7 December 1941, Honolulu, 8 a.m., the moment the Japanese air raid targeted Pearl Harbor.

6

U.S. STAMP DESIGNS OVER TIME
Cheryl R. Ganz

The tiny pieces of art we know as postage stamps tell many different stories. Their images chronicle political, business, and cultural changes over time. Stamps issued in the United States today look very different from those of 1847, the year the nation released its first prepaid postage stamps. They look different because the nation has changed and citizens see themselves in different ways. Stamps also look different because production and design techniques have evolved.

For a few years before the federal government issued stamps, some postmasters commissioned local printers to design and prepare stamps, known now as "postmaster provisionals." When Congress approved the postal act of 3 March 1847, the Post Office Department contracted with Rawdon, Wright, Hatch & Edson, a New York City engraving firm, to design and print the first stamps. The world's first postage stamp, England's Penny Black of 1840, featured a profile of Queen Victoria and set the design standard for early issues worldwide. To save on expenses, the postmaster general authorized a one-color, engraved printing. Postmaster General Cave Johnson initially instructed the firm to use a portrait of President Andrew Jackson on the 5¢ stamp and George Washington on the 10¢ denomination. However, the model, drawn in India ink and pencil, shows that Benjamin Franklin had replaced Jackson. Franklin's portrait, it was believed, would be more acceptable as a unifying icon for the tension-fraught nation because of his role in securing independence for the country (Figures 41 and 42).

Engravers employed by banknote companies designed stamps between 1847 and 1893, when the Bureau of Engraving and Printing won the production contract. Prior to 1893, the majority of images commemorated great American men. Emphasis expanded in 1893, when the Post Office observed Columbus's discovery of America with its first commemorative stamps. During the twentieth century's early decades, stamps became teaching tools, bearing images of pivotal U.S. historic events. Characterized by ornate frames, intense colors, and serif fonts, stamps of the period reflected the era's taste in design (Figure 43).

Like almost everything, stamp design changes with the times, accommodates improvements such as perforations and coils, mirrors the nation's fluid culture and sense of the aesthetic, and, of course, employs technological innovations. Art deco's streamlined contours, which expressed America's post–World War I optimism, appeared in stamp designs of the 1930s. This is evident in stamps released during Franklin D. Roosevelt's presidency. Lighter colors, sans serif fonts, and optional frames projected a sense of progress during the Great Depression. Subject matter reflected the period's concerns while reinforcing ideas of modernism and, during World War II, military prowess.

For well over a century, engravers and designers created the beautiful images seen on postage stamps. The bureau used various presses and techniques to achieve desired effects. Engraving is still used to produce some stamps, but high costs limit the frequency of its use. Other techniques, especially digital artistry, now dominate the field. Computers and computerized printing presses have definitely changed the look of stamps, allowing artists more freedom, a full palette of colors, and custom typography. And the images they create for stamps celebrate a far wider range of topics and themes, including popular culture, holidays, and sports.

Regardless of the subject, a stamp's illustration must be simple and eye-catching. It must stand out from its background and reduce well, and it must leave space for letters and numbers. It is the designer's responsibility to fulfill these requirements. Though tiny, a postage stamp is a work of art with a big story to tell.

FIGURE 41

The first U.S. stamps, printed in 1847, honored two of the nation's founding fathers. The 5¢ stamp featured a portrait of Benjamin Franklin.

FIGURE 42

The 10¢ stamp honored George Washington.

CONTENT: *1847* *1893*

Early stamps usually depicted famous **historical figures** including:

- *founding fathers*
- *presidents*
- *statesmen*
- *military officers*

24c George Washington, 1862
15c Abraham Lincoln, 1866
24c General Winfield Scott, 1893

DESIGN: *1847* *1933*

The design of early stamps was typically very **ornate** with:

- *one or two colors in rich hues*
- *serif fonts*
- *fancy frames*

3c George Washington, 1851
1c Benjamin Franklin, 1861
$5 John Marshall, 1903

PRODUCTION: *1847* *1914*

Early stamps were produced on **flat plate presses**:

- *recessed engraving produced a sharp image*
- *the later addition of perforations enabled easy separation*

24c Declaration of Independence, 1869
10c Fast Ocean Navigation, 1901
10c Louisiana Purchase Map, 1904

FIGURE 43
U.S. stamp design timeline.

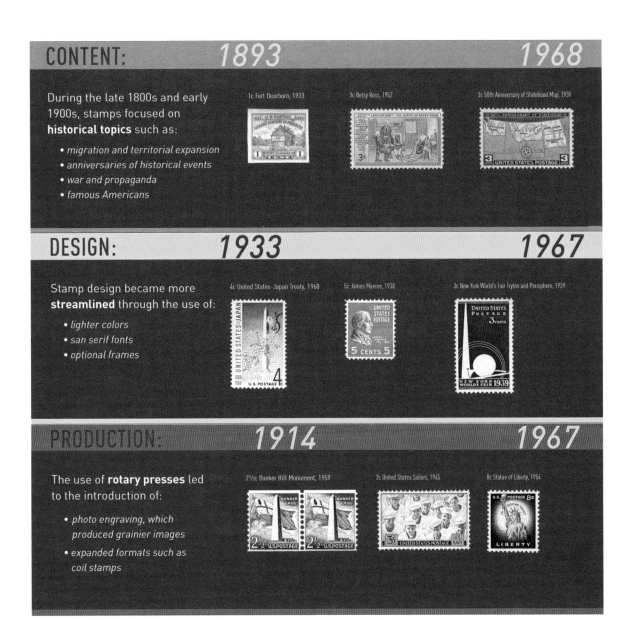

CONTENT: *1893*   *1968*

During the late 1800s and early
1900s, stamps focused on
historical topics such as:

- *migration and territorial expansion*
- *anniversaries of historical events*
- *war and propaganda*
- *famous Americans*

1c Fort Dearborn, 1933   3c Betsy Ross, 1952   3c 50th Anniversary of Statehood Map, 1939

DESIGN: *1933*   *1967*

Stamp design became more
streamlined through the use of:

- *lighter colors*
- *san serif fonts*
- *optional frames*

4c United States–Japan Treaty, 1960   5c James Monroe, 1938   3c New York World's Fair Trylon and Perisphere, 1939

PRODUCTION: *1914*   *1967*

The use of **rotary presses** led
to the introduction of:

- *photo engraving, which
  produced grainier images*
- *expanded formats such as
  coil stamps*

2½c Bunker Hill Monument, 1959   3c United States Sailors, 1945   8c Statue of Liberty, 1954

FIGURE 43
(*continued*)

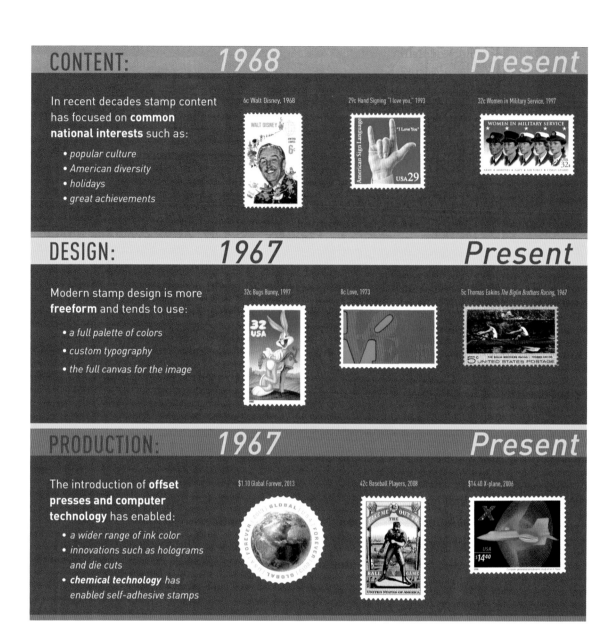

CONTENT: 1968 — Present

In recent decades stamp content has focused on **common national interests** such as:

- *popular culture*
- *American diversity*
- *holidays*
- *great achievements*

6c Walt Disney, 1968

29c Hand Signing "I love you," 1993

32c Women in Military Service, 1997

DESIGN: 1967 — Present

Modern stamp design is more **freeform** and tends to use:

- *a full palette of colors*
- *custom typography*
- *the full canvas for the image*

32c Bugs Bunny, 1997

8c Love, 1973

5c Thomas Eakins *The Biglin Brothers Racing*, 1967

PRODUCTION: 1967 — Present

The introduction of **offset presses and computer technology** has enabled:

- *a wider range of ink color*
- *innovations such as holograms and die cuts*
- ***chemical technology** has enabled self-adhesive stamps*

$1.10 Global Forever, 2013

42c Baseball Players, 2008

$14.40 X-plane, 2006

FIGURE 43
(*continued*)

7

THE POSTMASTER GENERAL'S COLLECTION

Cheryl R. Ganz and Daniel A. Piazza

The Postmaster General's Collection of the United States Postal Service (USPS) began in the 1860s as a modest set of Post Office Department (POD) files. Over time it has become a one-of-a-kind philatelic resource with unusual, rare, and unique holdings. It contains original artwork for rejected and approved stamp designs and postal stationery, stamps in full panes dating from the nineteenth century, color proofs, uncut press sheets, and historic artifacts such as the mail pouch the Apollo 15 astronauts carried to the Moon (Figures 44 and 45). Since 2010, it has been on long-term loan to the Smithsonian National Postal Museum.

To specialists, the Postmaster General's Collection is best known for its extensive holding of proofs made from the steel dies onto which stamp designs are engraved. In some cases, these proofs are *color trials*, impressions of the same engraving in different colors, made so that postal officials could select the best likeness. In other cases, the proofs are *progressive*, showing the vignette without the lettering and vice versa. These proofs demonstrate how different colors and the presence or absence of text can convey different meanings (Figure 46).

It is interesting to note that the practice of preparing a die proof for the postmaster general's approval continued long after engraving ceased to be the dominant method of stamp production. It survived the transition to private printers. Many of these "die proofs" are for stamps printed by photographic processes, for which no engraved die ever existed. They have been cut and mounted on a card countersunk with an impression to resemble a true large die proof. Since few die proofs later than the early 1960s are in private hands, this is never-before-seen material.

The collection's greatest strength lies in the behind-the-scenes stages of stamp production, representing different formats, layouts, and new printing methods used to print U.S. stamps since the mid-twentieth century. Scholars can trace an individual postage stamp issue from design through production and learn new information about the artwork concepts and the changes in production and approvals. Many rejected designs and printing color options have never been seen before. In addition, the collection is a great resource for tracing the changes over time in stamp design for content, production techniques, and artistic styles (Figures 47–49).

The collection also includes original artwork for postage stamps, with sketches and production materials that show how during the past seventy-five years a design evolved between the artist and the POD or USPS art director. The many art-concept submissions for the Elvis Presley and Marilyn Monroe stamps show the challenges that the USPS faced to find just the right image and to have it created in the most appropriate medium for that subject. The public voted on the two final Elvis artworks in a popular media campaign. The winning design became the best-selling postage stamp in the United States to date.

Now that this material resides at the Smithsonian National Postal Museum, students of U.S. philately are afforded the opportunity for a "close encounter" with archival material related to their area of special interest. Recently, philatelic scholars in a seminar course were able to study the original artwork, die proofs, and plate proofs for the Great Americans series, including several unissued stamps (Figure 50). The study of the Postmaster General's Collection, combined with research in other museum designer files and the Third Assistant Postmaster General design files for the early twentieth century, make the National Philatelic Collection a philatelic research destination.

FIGURE 44

This trial color proof shows the 15¢ Frederick Douglass stamp from the 1965–78
Prominent Americans series in a handsome purple shade. The stamp was issued in
magenta instead. Courtesy of the United States Postal Service, Postmaster General's
Collection.

**For Approval of Engraving and Provisional
Approval of the Color:
Final color approval to be given on Press Sheet.**

Postmaster General

FIGURE 45

A proof of the "Amedeo" spelling error on the 21¢ Amadeo P. Giannini stamp from the
Prominent Americans series. The error made it all the way to the postmaster general—
who approved it for printing—before it was discovered and the stamp reengraved.
Courtesy of the United States Postal Service, Postmaster General's Collection.

For Approval of Engraving and Provisional
Approval of the Color:
Final color approval to be given on Press Sheet

FIGURE 46
Sojourner Truth, a former slave and
freedom orator, was honored in 1986 in
the Black Heritage series. Postmaster
General Albert V. Casey approved this 22¢
proof. Courtesy of the United States Postal
Service, Postmaster General's Collection.

FIGURE 47

The 1998 Breast Cancer Research stamp's purchase price includes a surcharge that has raised over $72 million for research. The stamp's designer, Ethel Kessler, is a breast cancer survivor. Illustrator Whitney Sherman created this dramatic artwork of a mythical goddess of the hunt. Courtesy of the United States Postal Service, Postmaster General's Collection.

FIGURE 48

Merengue is a Caribbean dance in the 2005 Let's Dance commemorative series, painted by Rafael Lopez. Courtesy of the United States Postal Service, Postmaster General's Collection.

FIGURE 49

Kam Mak's oil painting of a Chinese Lion
Dance head celebrates Chinatown parades
on the 42¢ Lunar New Year stamp for 2009,
the Year of the Ox. Courtesy of the United
States Postal Service, Postmaster General's
Collection.

FIGURE 50
Curator Daniel A. Piazza (right) and researcher Jay Stotts study original artwork for an unissued Jefferson Davis stamp in the 1980–85 Great Americans series and the 20¢ Harry S. Truman stamp of 1984 that replaced it.

8

THE BENJAMIN K. MILLER COLLECTION
Cheryl R. Ganz

The Benjamin K. Miller Collection tells two great stories, one of Miller himself and the other of his fabled collection. The collection is on loan to the Smithsonian National Postal Museum from The New York Public Library, Astor, Lenox and Tilden Foundations.

Until middle age, travel, research, and writing fascinated Milwaukee attorney Benjamin Kurtz Miller (1857–1928). He also enjoyed a casual interest in philately. Then in 1918, when Miller bought one of the famous "Inverted Jenny" stamps discovered that year by William T. Robey, philately became Miller's obsession. He immediately set a goal of owning one example of every U.S. postage stamp known in his day, an objective he nearly achieved in the early 1920s (Figures 51 and 52).

Besides one example of every U.S. postage stamp, Miller also collected rare grills, special printings, all coil and vending machine examples, and back-of-the-book issues. He collected many varieties, two-color shades, frauds and forgeries, fresh unused stamps, and varied cancellations. In addition, he sought bisects, errors, and special-use stamps. And he enjoyed "plating" stamps, seeking one copy for each position on a printing plate (Figure 53).

To complete his grill collection, Miller purchased the William L. Stevenson collection of grilled stamps (Figure 54). The grill impression, a waffle-like pattern, was embossed into the paper of the stamp to prevent stamp reuse (Figure 55). Stevenson had categorized the experimental impressions. His system of assigning each variety a letter of the alphabet is still followed today. When Miller obtained the 1¢ Z grill, no other examples were known. Hence, it set Miller's collection apart from all others. Since then, another 1¢ Z grill has surfaced and is in private hands. Many collectors consider the Z grill on the 1¢ blue Franklin to be America's rarest stamp.

In 1925, with the intention that it be a teaching tool, Benjamin K. Miller donated his legendary collection of U.S. postage stamps (1847 to the 1920s) to The New York Public Library. The library displayed the collection for more than fifty years, inspiring generations of collectors. After the theft of numerous valuable items in 1977, the library locked the collection away. More than half the stolen objects were recovered during the 1980s.

Thirty-five years after the theft, New York stamp auctioneer Scott Trepel spotted two of the stolen Miller stamps in an auction lot. They were the two famous inverted stamp errors of the 1869 engraved series: the 15¢ design with the Landing of Columbus printed upside down and the 30¢ design of the Eagle and Shield with the flags printed upside down (Figures 56 and 57). Soon after printing, both had escaped to a post office for sale. The two have been returned to Miller's original album pages. Miller's obituary in *Mekeel's Weekly Stamp News* in 1928 noted that the 30¢ invert of 1869 was the most valuable stamp in Miller's collection. Since then, many other stamps and covers in his collection have surpassed this stamp in rarity and value.

Through a generous loan from The New York Public Library to the Smithsonian National Postal Museum, the Benjamin K. Miller Collection is once again an inspiration to collectors. Millions have seen the collection on exhibit at the Smithsonian National Postal Museum; still more have studied it online and read the many articles and book. Benjamin K. Miller could not have imagined the impact his remarkable achievement and generosity have made on the philatelic community.

FIGURE 51

Benjamin K. Miller plated the 10¢ Washington stamp of 1847. He tried to find every plate location of the issue and often on cover, such as this pair of 57 and 58 left positions. Courtesy of The New York Public Library, Astor, Lenox and Tilden Foundations.

FIGURE 52

Miller acquired early and rare coil varieties, including this 1911 example on cover known as the 3¢ Orangeburg coil. Courtesy of The New York Public Library, Astor, Lenox and Tilden Foundations.

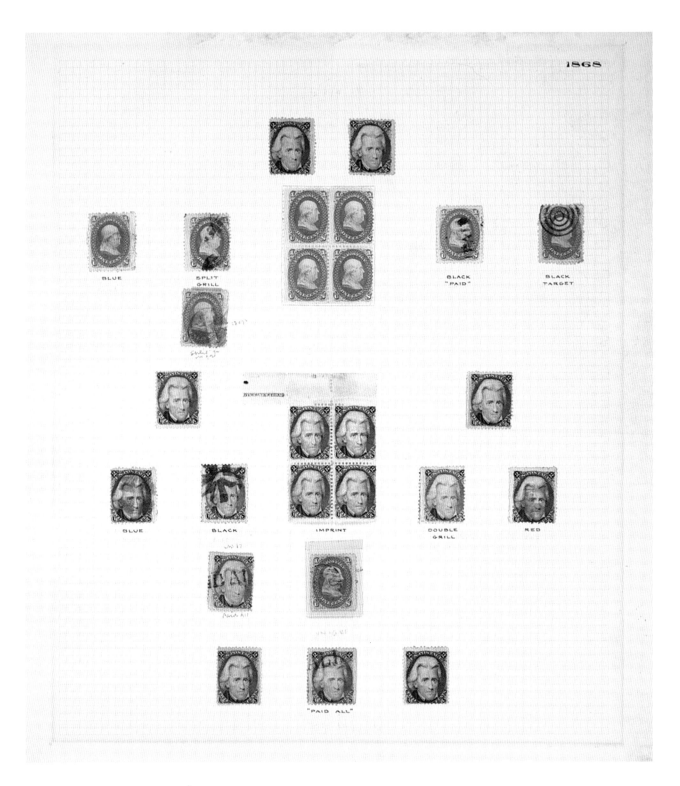

FIGURE 53

Miller's album page of 1868 issues includes the 2¢ Andrew Jackson, known as the Black Jack, and the 1¢ Franklin, including the rare 1¢ Z grill (bottom center). Courtesy of The New York Public Library, Astor, Lenox and Tilden Foundations.

FIGURE 54

Miller acquired the 1¢ Z grill in 1923
in a private purchase of the William L.
Stevenson grill collection. Many consider
it the rarest U.S. postage stamp. Only two
are known. Courtesy of The New York
Public Library, Astor, Lenox and Tilden
Foundations.

FIGURE 55

The reverse of the 1¢ Z grill shows the grill
impression, a waffle-like pattern embossed
into the paper of the stamp. The Z
differentiates this grill's characteristics and
dimensions from other grills. Courtesy of
The New York Public Library, Astor, Lenox
and Tilden Foundations.

FIGURE 56

One of the rarities of the 1869 pictorial issue is the 30¢ Shield, Eagle, and Flags invert, shown here before the 1977 theft. Courtesy of The New York Public Library, Astor, Lenox and Tilden Foundations.

FIGURE 57

The recovered Miller example of the 30¢ Shield, Eagle, and Flags invert single, thirty-five years after the theft. Courtesy of The New York Public Library, Astor, Lenox and Tilden Foundations.

9

U.S. REVENUES
Ronald E. Lesher

The stories and stamps of levying taxes and establishing fees for government services intrigue many collectors. The usually beautiful revenue stamps can indicate that a tax has been paid or will be paid or perhaps that an object is tax exempt, that a fee for service was paid, or that one has a credit with the government. Between 1954 and 1977, the Internal Revenue Service transferred approximately 1,900 varieties of obsolete revenue stamps to the Smithsonian, now a fascinating segment of the National Philatelic Collection's holdings.

As the Civil War accelerated and the flood of expenditures threatened the Union's financial viability, Congress passed the Revenue Act of 1862, which established the U.S. Internal Revenue Service and initiated the use of adhesive revenue stamps. George S. Boutwell, the first commissioner of internal revenue, sought bids from security printers for the design and production of revenue stamps. Philadelphia-based Butler & Carpenter won the first contract to print the stamps.

One of the prized objects in the National Philatelic Collection's holdings is a black, leather-bound album consisting of twenty-one double-sided pages of proofs of the revenue stamps printed by Butler & Carpenter from 1862 to 1872. Joseph R. Carpenter presented this album to George S. Boutwell in 1873, when Boutwell left his position as U.S. Secretary of the Treasury (Figure 58).

Documentary stamps were used on legal documents such as agreements, contracts, and mortgages, often involving the transfer of ownership of real property, stocks, and bonds. The $500 documentary stamp of 1871, one of the "Persian Rug" designs, is easily the most recognizable revenue stamp because of its intricate beauty and three-color printing. During the late 1860s and early 1870s, the taxes due on a mortgage were determined at the rate of 50¢ per $500. To pay the taxes due, the Morris & Essex Rail Road mortgage of $5 million was stamped with ten of these Persian Rugs (Figure 59).

The size of the mortgage of the Morris & Essex Rail Road was not that unusual, so the Internal Revenue Service asked the Joseph Carpenter firm to prepare a design for a $5,000 documentary stamp, which would take up less space on the mortgage papers than ten of the $500 Persian Rugs. The result was another fabulous stamp, approved in June 1872. The Internal Revenue Service never ordered the $5,000 stamps, and the taxes for which the high denomination would have been used were eliminated three months later (Figure 60).

Many commodities, including patent medicines, photographs, perfumes, chewing gum, tooth powder, toiletries, playing cards, tobacco products, and alcohol, have also been taxed. When the first beer stamps were needed in 1866, the Note Printing Division of the U.S. Treasury created stamps for the permitted sizes of beer: eighth, sixth, quarter, half, and one barrel and one hogshead (two barrels in volume). California brewers wanted and demanded the third-barrel stamp. The brewers knew that the maximum load that mules could bear was two of the third size barrels. Although never issued in the Series of 1866, the third barrel was included in the Series of 1867 by the Note Printing Division (Figure 61).

The use of revenue stamps slowed during the 1950s, and by the late 1960s few remained. More efficient means of collecting revenue were introduced. Nevertheless, a few tax stamps remain in use today, including the familiar migratory bird hunting stamps known as "Duck Stamps" and the firearms transfer tax stamps (Figure 62).

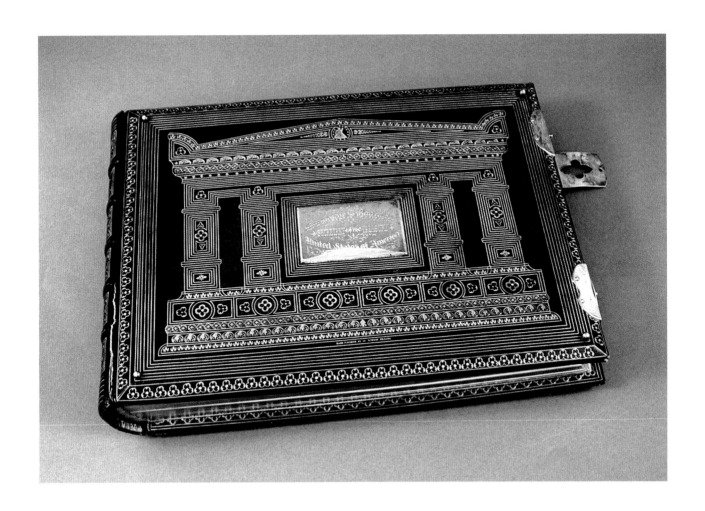

FIGURE 58

Presentation album of revenue proofs
presented to George S. Boutwell in 1873,
when he left his position as U.S. Secretary
of the Treasury.

FIGURE 59

The $500 documentary stamp of 1872 is popularly known as the "Persian Rug."

FIGURE 60

The $5,000 Persian Rug was approved for
use on large mortgages ($5 million and
higher), but no stamps were ever delivered.

FIGURE 61
The 1866 third-barrel essay for beer was not a permitted size in the 1866 law, but California brewers insisted upon it.

FIGURE 62
The $15 Black Scoters Duck Stamp of 2003 with added original artwork, known as a remarque, by artist Joseph Hautman.

10

HISTORY OF U.S. POSTAL OPERATIONS
Nancy A. Pope

The nation's founding fathers recognized the necessity of the postal system and provided for it in the Constitution: "The Congress shall have Power To . . . establish Post Offices and post Roads" (U.S. Constitution, Article 1, Section 8). Over time, as the nation changed, postal services changed, always making American life and business more efficient. Although the system's size and breadth alone would have made it a major factor in national growth, congressional use of the service to further a variety of aims heightened its impact. Postal funds have sustained and created transportation systems. Post offices signaled the establishment of frontier communities. Congress used its postal powers as a tool to expand the nation by encouraging road building into sparsely populated areas, which, in turn, encouraged migration. This significant history is observed through an array of objects in the National Philatelic Collection that showcase the U.S. postal system's history and illustrate its importance. The collection's maps, postal act documents, and stagecoach contracts, for instance, breathe life into the system's early role in helping build the nation (Figure 63).

The high cost of letters kept their numbers down through the early nineteenth century. A series of postal reforms in the 1840s and 1850s began the transformation of the system from a tool to inform the citizenry (through low newspaper rates) into one that encouraged that citizenry to communicate on its own. The first U.S. stamps appeared in 1847, after the postal reform of 1845 balanced cheap postage with economies of scale. Another reduction in postage in 1851 made the system even more affordable. Further encouragements included the establishment of free delivery to homes (beginning in 1863 for select northern cities and 1896 as an experiment in rural areas), money orders (1863), parcel post (1913), and even banking (1911–1967). Numerous items in the museum's collections illuminate this transformation, from rural wagons and the tools used by early rural carriers for their daily rounds to some of the packages they delivered, money orders, and postal savings certificates.

As the variety and eras of sorting units in the museum demonstrate, the core aspect of mail processing remained remarkably the same until the mid-twentieth century. Postal employees continued to separate mail into pigeon-hole sorting units (Figure 64). The Post Office Department, hamstrung by budget constraints during the Great Depression and World War II, entered the 1950s facing a potential system collapse unless mail could be moved out of post offices as quickly as it flowed in.

A major advance integrated the postage stamp into the mechanization process. Manufacturers added fluorescent "tagging" materials to stamps that although invisible to the naked eye, triggered processing machines to "face" or maneuver each envelope so that it entered into machines called "facer/cancellers" in the right direction for cancellation. Several of the museum's stamps help track the style and variety of tagging used during the early years of the practice (Figure 65).

The transformative key to improving mail processing came in 1963 with the addition of the five-digit Zoning Improvement Plan (also known as zip code) system (Figure 66). Clerks entered parts of this code into machines such as the multiposition letter sorting machine (MPLSM), allowing letter mail to be processed far more quickly and efficiently. As mail processing technology advanced, zip codes were rendered into machine-readable barcodes (Figure 67). The codes evolved into the United States Postal Service's Intelligent Mail barcode (IMb) system. By the early twenty-first century, thirty-one digits of information were used on mail, providing data that revealed how the mail was presorted, whether it was first class mail or a periodical, the business sending each piece, and automatic address-forwarding information. When preaddressed business reply mail was returned, businesses could forecast its arrival time and estimate how much money was coming in.

The U.S. Postal Service faces daunting challenges in the upcoming decades. Even though email, texting, and online bill paying have replaced much first class mail, the number of addresses receiving mail steadily grows. Discussions over the service's future include issues such as privatization (partial or total), limiting universal service (including closing post offices), and pricing levels. Resolution of these questions is critical to the long-term success of the service.

FIGURE 63

Commercial aviation owes its existence to the Post Office. After 1926, postal-funded aircraft, trained pilots, and a transcontinental flyway became the nucleus of privately owned airlines. Mail cargo fees kept companies in business until passenger traffic was supportable in the late 1930s.

FIGURE 64

Sorting unit owned by Postmaster John T. Jackson of Alanthus, Virginia. The pigeon hole sorting system seen here was at the core of mail processing until the mid-twentieth century.

FIGURE 65

The 5¢ 1963 City Mail Delivery issue was
the first commemorative stamp produced
as a tagged stamp for mail processing, as
shown here under ultraviolet light before
and after tagging.

FIGURE 66

Mr. Zip became the friendly icon used by postal officials to remind people to use zip codes on their mail. Although required on commercial mail for rate benefits, zip codes were never required for private use.

FIGURE 67

The barcode shown here is the POSTNET code. It bridged the gap between zip codes and Intelligent Mail barcodes and was sprayed on envelopes during the postal sorting process.

Terry and Connie Moser
114 Cedar Hollow Dr North
Fort Mill, SC 29715

CLEARED

Honorable Vice President Richard Cheney
The White House
1600 Pennsylvania Avenue N.W.
Washington, DC 20500

11

MAIL MARKS HISTORY
Cheryl R. Ganz and Daniel A. Piazza

Stamps and markings on mail reveal how it was transported and what challenges it encountered. The effort to move mail ever farther and faster contributed to major advances in transportation technology—from bicycles to trains, canoes to submarines, balloons to spacecraft. Times of difficulty sparked innovations in mail delivery. How did mail travel? What route did it take to reach its final destination? How long did it take? What obstacles did the mail encounter along the way? Different kinds of markings on mail reconstruct the story. Postage rates show what services were requested. Postmarks record where and when mail entered and traveled through the system. Auxiliary markings give routing directions or indicate special services. Addresses and handwriting provide information about both sender and recipient. The envelope's condition delivers clues to handling (Figures 68 and 69).

Mail has been delivered in a surprising variety of ways on both land and sea. The origins of modern postal systems date to the thirteenth century, when private couriers carried dispatches for governments, churches, universities, and other institutions. Over time, these private systems opened to the public. As populations grew, people tried moving the mail using a range of transportation technologies. Ocean-going ships have transported mail from one continent to another since at least the 1300s. Steamships, introduced in the 1830s, shortened Atlantic Ocean crossings to a little more than two weeks. Over time, more and more steamship companies secured contracts to carry government mail. By the mid-1860s, government mail contracts heavily subsidized the construction and operation of transatlantic passenger liners (Figure 70).

As cities expanded in size, so did methods of mail transport. Trains and buses carried mail over long distances. At the turn of the twentieth century, horse-drawn wagons and electric streetcars transported mail within most cities. By the 1920s, motorized postal trucks became the dominant form of urban mail transportation. In the United States, as railroads declined, the Post Office used buses and the new Interstate Highway System to move mail among cities and serve communities in between.

Aviation technology forever changed mail delivery in the United States and around the world. From the 1800s onward, a wide variety of aircraft and space-craft have carried the mail. Over the years, these craft have increased greatly in speed, size, sophistication, and endurance, revolutionizing global mail delivery. Markings on mail record the major transitions and milestones in airmail service that have occurred worldwide over the last two centuries (Figures 71, 72, and 73).

Balloons and gliders carried the first airmail. By the 1920s, zeppelins had established postal routes over long distances. On 17 December 1903 at Kitty Hawk, North Carolina, the Wright Flyer became the first powered, heavier-than-air machine to achieve controlled, sustained flight with a pilot aboard. As the twentieth century progressed, the speed and reliability of airplanes improved considerably and transformed communication, moving the mail more efficiently than ever. In the 1900s, scientists used balloons and rockets to explore the strato-sphere and space for the first time. Only a few of these space missions carried mail, either privately by astronauts or as payload. Markings on this mail docu-ment these early space explorations as well as later space flights and missions.

Wars, natural disasters, epidemics, and other types of adversity have an im-pact on mail, leaving behind objects that bear testament to history. Pieces of mail that survive challenging circumstances such as these provide evidence of how normal communications were disrupted and how postal authorities coped with formidable obstacles (Figures 74 and 75). With the help of innovative ideas, clever inventions, and persistence on the part of postal employees, the mail usu-ally managed to get through, even during the most difficult times.

FIGURE 68

The oldest paper letter in the National
Philatelic Collection, dated 1390, traveled
on the Silk Road. It discusses prices of
luxury fabrics and spices such as cinnamon
and pepper. Mailed by a Venetian merchant
in Damascus on 24 November 1390, it
was carried by courier to Beirut, where
it boarded a Venetian galley. It arrived in
Venice on 26 December, having traveled
1,650 miles in one month.

FIGURE 69

British naval lieutenant and entrepreneur Thomas Fletcher Waghorn pioneered an overland mail route between the Egyptian cities of Alexandria and Suez in order to speed up mail delivery between Great Britain and its empire in India. About 200 covers are known to have survived with the endorsement "Care of Mr. Waghorn," this example from 1838.

FIGURE 70

First-class *Titanic* passenger George E. Graham, a Canadian returning from a European buying trip for Eaton's department store, addressed this folded letter on ship's stationery. Destined for Berlin, it received *Titanic*'s onboard postmark ("Transatlantic Post Office 7") on 10 April 1912 and was sent ashore with the mail, probably at Cherbourg, France. Mail is one of the rarest artifacts from *Titanic*.

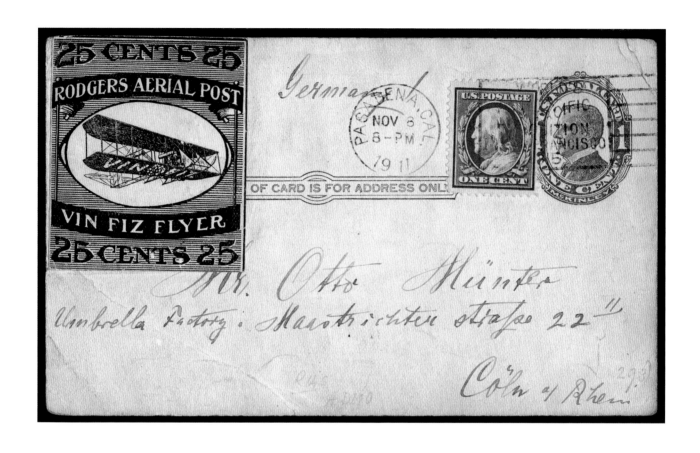

OF CARD IS FOR ADDRESS ONLY

FIGURE 71

This postal card traveled on the last legs
of the first transcontinental flight via the
Vin Fiz Flyer, piloted in 1911 by Calbraith
Perry Rodgers. The makers of the grape
soda Vin Fiz sponsored the flight, signaling
the use of the post for advertising. The
entire flight from Sheepshead Bay, New
York, to Long Beach, California, took
forty-nine days, including stops,
breakdowns, and crashes.

FIGURE 72

On 20–21 May 1932, Amelia Earhart became the first woman to pilot solo across the Atlantic Ocean, flying from Newfoundland to Ireland. The feat brought her worldwide acclaim and a place in aviation history. On her flight, Earhart carried fifty pieces of privately transported mail.

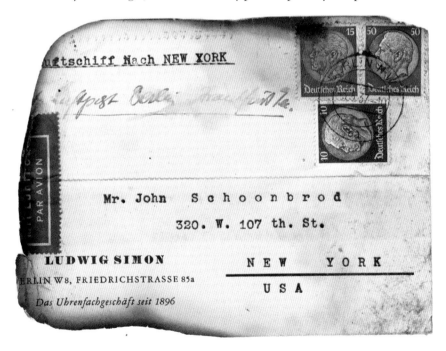

FIGURE 73

The 6 May 1937 *Hindenburg* disaster ended the golden era of airships. While attempting to land at Lakehurst, New Jersey, the airship burst into flames. Within thirty-four seconds, it was destroyed. Two-thirds of the passengers and crew survived, but most mail burned.

FIGURE 74

This pad of stamps survived the ferocious 1871 Chicago fire, which burned from 8 to 10 October. The fire destroyed about four square miles of the city, including the main post office, where these stamps were recovered.

FIGURE 75

Located at 90 Church Street, across the street from the World Trade Center, this mailbox was scratched, dented, and filled with dust on 11 September 2001, but its body and mail inside remained intact.

12

MILITARY MAIL
Lynn Heidelbaugh

Mail exchanged between military personnel in the field and the home front carries stories as varied as life itself. The posts provide a vital communication link for America's sons and daughters when they go to the front line. From the War of Independence to the present, mail has been strategic for the transmission of official information and for maintaining morale. Every effort is expended to ensure that the armed forces have access to the postal system (Figure 76).

The U.S. government supports and encourages military mail by making it simple to send. During the Civil War and Spanish-American War, the words "soldier's letter" written on an envelope allowed troops to send messages with no prepayment; postage was collected upon delivery. In 1917, Congress granted American forces in combat zones the right to send personal correspondence free of charge. For overseas mail, the Department of Defense subsidizes the system and provides for free mail from service personnel in designated areas, now determined by the U.S. Secretary of Defense (Figure 77).

The unique challenges of delivering mail to or from the battlefront, foreign outposts, and naval ships leave their mark on military mail. One such mark is the Army Post Office (APO) and Fleet Post Office (FPO) address. During World War I, officials developed the APO numbering system to provide flexible, secure, and accurate addresses for mail delivery to the deployed. World War II sorely tested the military mail system and prompted another innovation, V-mail, to handle the immense volume of mail. V-mail used standardized stationery and microfilm processing to produce lighter, smaller cargo to expedite overseas mail and free up space for critical supplies (Figure 78).

Charitable organizations have also left their mark on military mail. Deployed personnel frequently lacked adequate supplies of stationery, and organizations often filled the need by supplying writing materials. The logos of the American Red Cross, YMCA, Jewish Welfare League, and USO, to name a few, appear on preprinted postcards, letterhead, and envelopes that they distributed to the military (Figure 79). During the Civil War and World War I, those unable to write their own letters might dictate messages to volunteers visiting the hospitals. Volunteers also brought writing supplies to prisoner-of-war camps.

The contents of military mail have been influenced by the special circumstances. Censors looking for leaks of crucial information have reviewed prisoner-of-war letters in all wars fought by the United States (Figure 80). During World Wars I and II, unit commanders or censor clerks removed or blackened any suspicious information and then signed off on content using a special handstamp. Monitoring the morale level also fell to these censors, who recognized the central relationship between morale and communication with home.

The mail helps maintain civic ties and morale—hometown newspapers keep deployed personnel informed of events, and the mail has been instrumental during election years by delivering absentee ballots. As early as the Civil War, several Union and Confederate states used the mail for balloting. In 1864, the state of Ohio, for instance, created special envelopes for military personnel to cast ballots for the presidential and state elections (Figure 81).

Handling military mail has necessitated many specialized steps and materials. The reason that the military and postal service go to these lengths remains constant (Figure 82). A ready and reliable mail system helps keep the armed forces engaged, secure, and strong.

FIGURE 76

The duplex handstamp salvaged from the battleship USS *Oklahoma* shows the last date of its use, on 6 December 1941, the day before Japan attacked Pearl Harbor.

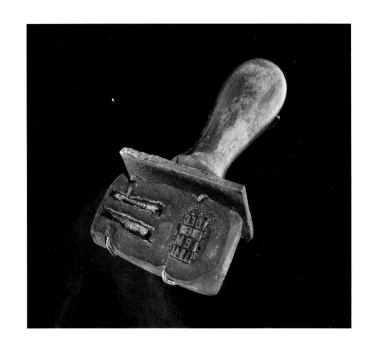

FIGURE 77

A U.S. Marine Corps lieutenant fashioned a postcard from food packaging and marked the corner "Free Mail" at the start of the war in Afghanistan.

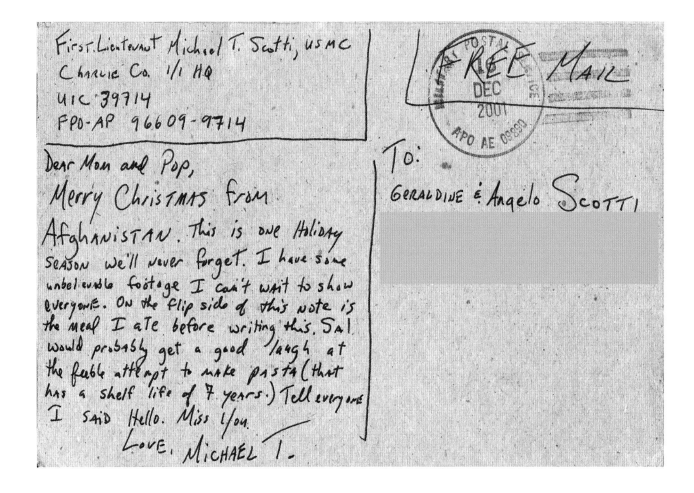

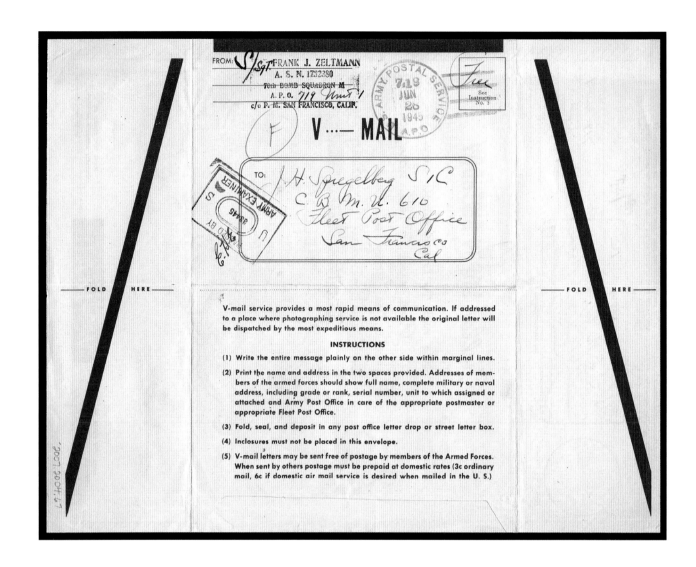

FROM: S/Sgt. FRANK J. ZELTMANN
A. S. N. 1232380
76th BOMB SQUADRON M
A. P. O. 719 Unit 1
c/o P. M. SAN FRANCISCO, CALIF.

V ····— MAIL

TO: J. H. Spiegelberg S/C
C. B. M. U. 610
Fleet Post Office
San Francisco
Cal

V-mail service provides a most rapid means of communication. If addressed
to a place where photographing service is not available the original letter will
be dispatched by the most expeditious means.

INSTRUCTIONS

(1) Write the entire message plainly on the other side within marginal lines.

(2) Print the name and address in the two spaces provided. Addresses of members of the armed forces should show full name, complete military or naval
address, including grade or rank, serial number, unit to which assigned or
attached and Army Post Office in care of the appropriate postmaster or
appropriate Fleet Post Office.

(3) Fold, seal, and deposit in any post office letter drop or street letter box.

(4) Inclosures must not be placed in this envelope.

(5) V-mail letters may be sent free of postage by members of the Armed Forces.
When sent by others postage must be prepaid at domestic rates (3c ordinary
mail, 6c if domestic air mail service is desired when mailed in the U. S.)

FIGURE 78

Whether shipped in its original lightweight
format or transferred onto microfilm,
V-mail was designed for airmail transport.

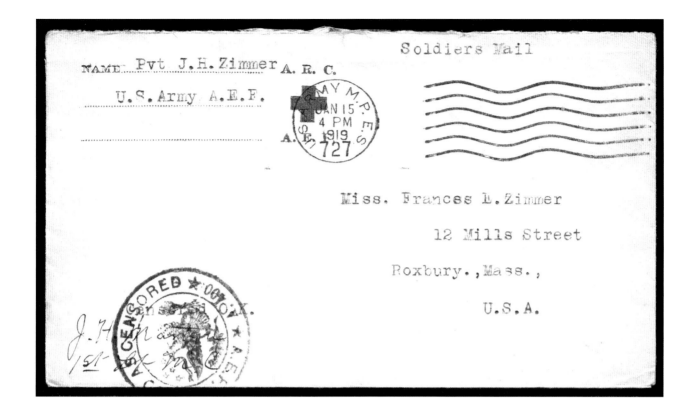

FIGURE 79

The American Red Cross helped in many ways during World War I, including providing stationery and transcribing letters for injured military personnel.

FIGURE 80

Censors marked "Examined" in the top left corner and "Prisoner of war" at the bottom of this Civil War cover.

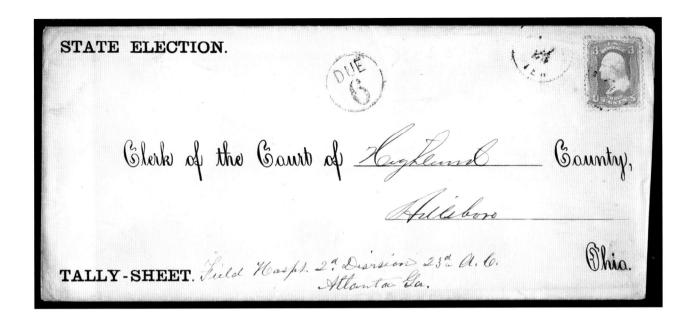

STATE ELECTION.

Clerk of the Court of Highland County,

Hillsboro

Ohio.

TALLY-SHEET. *Field Hospt. 2d Division 23d A. C.*
Atlanta Ga.

FIGURE 81

This envelope mailed from a Union Army field hospital contained a tally sheet recording the votes of Highland County soldiers for the 1864 Ohio state election.

FIGURE 82

This 1960s mailbox served the crew of USNS *General Simon B. Buckner*, which took part in a major operation for Korea and also transported troops for Vietnam.

13

HAWAII

Cheryl R. Ganz

Hawaii's postage stamps rouse more excitement than those of nearly all other countries. Romantic stories surround their printings and uses, and since the hobby's beginning in the mid-nineteenth century, collectors have feverishly sought them. The National Philatelic Collection includes singles of each of Hawaii's stamp issues, including the rare and fragile Missionaries (Figures 83 and 84). In addition, the collection includes artwork, die proofs, stationery, and correspondence donated by the American Bank Note Company. The Missionaries, Hawaii's first four stamps, are particularly enchanting. Printed in 1851, the stamps' primitive designs invoke images of the islands' simple, exotic life—a virtual paradise. Their rarity, that missionaries and very early businessmen used them, and the myths surrounding them all heighten their appeal. As a group, the stamps of Hawaii document a fascinating history, chronicling the islands' rulers and journey through three forms of government—kingdom, provisional government, and republic—before being annexed as a U.S. territory in 1898. All three pre-U.S. governments issued stamps.

James Cook made the first recorded stop by a European on the islands in 1778. He named the islands the Sandwich Islands after his benefactor, the Earl of Sandwich. The islands quickly became a winter port for Pacific whaling vessels. Devastated by smallpox and in the interests of self-preservation, in 1810 the Hawaiian Islands unified into a royal kingdom under the leadership of Kamehameha I, a powerful and convincing tribal leader. Within a decade, missionaries from the United States appeared. Besides building schools and converting natives to Christianity, they established the first sugar plantation in 1835.

The Hawaiian Post Office originated with planters and missionaries who wanted to communicate with their families, religious leaders, and business associates. A postal treaty was signed with the United States in 1849, and mailbag exchanges with the San Francisco Post Office began the next year. The kingdom's first stamps, the Missionaries, were used on international mail, particularly to the United States. In 1864, Hawaii contracted with the National Bank Note Company to print its stamps, which featured portraits of the kingdom's royalty (Figures 85, 86, and 87). In 1879, National merged with American Bank Note Company, where printing of Hawaiian stamps continued without interruption until annexation.

Queen Liliuokalani, Hawaii's last monarch, relinquished her throne in 1893, and the United States annexed Hawaii in 1898 (Figure 88). During the interim, Hawaii continued issuing stamps. The temporary government overprinted the remaining stamps from the Kingdom of Hawaii with "Provisional Government." When it became clear that the United States would not immediately annex Hawaii, in 1894 the newly established Republic of Hawaii issued postage stamps and, two years later, stamps for its Foreign Affairs Department. Use of the Republic issues continued after annexation, until a territorial government was established on 14 June 1900.

The National Philatelic Collection has many objects from the territorial and statehood eras of Hawaii as well. Stamp imagery of surfing and Aloha shirts reinforce the idea of the islands as paradise. Coconuts with messages sent home by post boast of the exotic setting. Mail demonstrates how the strategic location of Hawaii made it a stop in the first airmail routes across the Pacific. One amazing piece of mail was postmarked in Honolulu at the very moment of the Japanese attack on Pearl Harbor that brought the United States into World War II. Hawaii became the fiftieth state in 1959.

FIGURE 83

A. H. Spencer wrote from his East Maui plantation, "This is but a small speck in the world and it is very dull times." His letter departed 22 January 1853 on the *Excel* and arrived in San Francisco on 18 February. The black "Ship 6" indicates that U.S. postage was collected from the recipient.

FIGURE 84

In 1905, a workman salvaged this envelope,
written by William Dawson, with other
old letters from the charred remains inside
a furnace in an abandoned tannery. The
unique strip of three 13¢ Missionaries, Types
I, II, I, on this triple-rate cover illustrates
the arrangement of the two typeset clichés,
or designs, on the printing plate.

FIGURE 85

This 1860 cover mailed to New York bears
a 5¢ Kamehameha III stamp for Hawaiian
postage along with a 12¢ Washington
stamp to cover the 2¢ ship fee and 10¢
transcontinental rate. It weighed one
ounce at the San Francisco Post Office. The
manuscript "Due 10" was added to collect
the shortage from the recipient.

FIGURE 86

In 1889, to fill requests from collectors, the Post Office ordered the American Bank Note Company to reprint the 1853 Kamehameha III stamps. This specimen sheet is from the printer's archive.

only impression   2620.

FIGURE 87

In 1894, the American Bank Note
Company made only one impression
of this die proof of the statue of King
Kamehameha I, who united Hawaii into a
kingdom. Located across from the Iolani
Palace, it is draped with flowered leis each
11 June to honor the first king.

FIGURE 88

The 2¢ Queen Liliuokalani stamp of 1890–
91 was the first postage stamp to depict a
butterfly.

14

CANAL ZONE AND THE MISSING BRIDGE ERROR
Richard Bates

Those who collect stamps and postal history of the Canal Zone tell many stories related to their philatelic passion. One story, however, tops them all—the story of the Thatcher Ferry Bridge error. Details of this story and many others are preserved in the files of the Canal Zone Postal Service, now housed at the Smithsonian National Postal Museum. The extensive holdings provide scholars and philatelists an opportunity to study the evolution of a postage stamp from concept through actual usage.

The Panama Canal Treaty signed in 1977 ended United States control of the canal. Six years later, the Canal Zone Postal Service collection of over 100,000 philatelic items and postal archives was transferred to the Smithsonian Institution. The extensive collection and archives include design materials, essays, approved die proofs, plate proofs, and press sheets for postage stamps and postal stationery produced by the United States Bureau of Engraving and Printing beginning in 1928, when the Canal Zone began issuing stamps of its own design. Earlier, United States or Panama stamps overprinted CANAL ZONE had been used. The holding also includes artifacts related to the functioning of the Canal Zone Postal Service, such as the dies used to produce or revalue postal stationery and the twenty-five-subject rubber handstamp wrapped around a rolling pin. The postmaster used a rolling pin from his kitchen to apply one type of CRISTOBAL CANAL ZONE precancel, a stamp canceled prior to affixing on mail matter (Figures 89 and 90).

On 12 October 1962, the Thatcher Ferry Bridge opened across the Panama Canal. In celebration, the Canal Zone Postal Service issued a commemorative postage stamp depicting the new bridge (Figures 91, 92, and 93). The Bureau of Engraving and Printing in Washington, D.C., used the Giori press for two passes, the second superimposing a silver bridge over the map of the Western Hemisphere in black. The Bureau printed 775,000 stamps. In a printing error, one sheet lacked the silver bridge. One pane of four from this "missing bridge" sheet escaped detection. The Canal Zone Postal Service sold it unknowingly to Boston stamp dealer H. E. Harris as part of a larger order. He soon inquired about buying more (Figures 94 and 95).

The Canal Zone philatelic agency had realized that some stamps had no silver bridge and announced the deliberate reprinting of the missing bridge stamps, similar to the reprinting of the Dag Hammarskjold inverted color error ordered by the United States Post Office Department earlier that year. Harris filed a preliminary injunction to prevent the reprinting. Following lengthy litigation, Canal Zone authorities agreed not to reprint the error and to destroy the upper left "discovery" pane. The two unsold panes were laminated in plastic to comply with the legal settlement. The Smithsonian Institution received the lower left pane in a 1966 transfer to its National Philatelic Collection (Figure 96). The lower right pane was placed in the Canal Zone Museum. The Canal Zone pane transferred to the Smithsonian with the Canal Zone postal collection and archives in 1983. The Harris pane was broken up and is in the hands of the public.

The 4¢ "Missing Bridge" error occupies a unique place in philately. The agreement not to intentionally reproduce additional quantities of this or any other error produced by the bureau forever changed the landscape of philately and ensured that the upper right pane retained value as a great philatelic rarity.

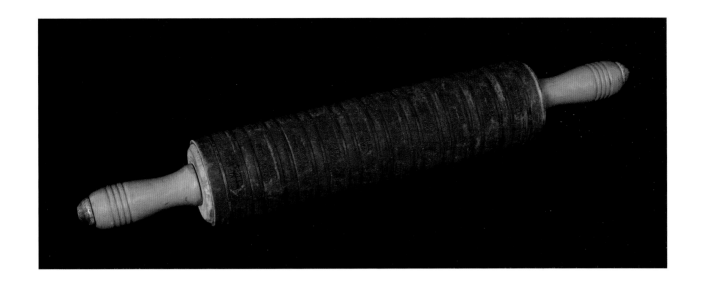

FIGURE 89

Rolling pin with fifty-subject rubber
handstamp used to apply the
CRISTOBAL CANAL ZONE precancel to
commemorative-size stamps.

FIGURE 90

The CRISTOBAL CANAL ZONE

precancel on a commemorative-size stamp.

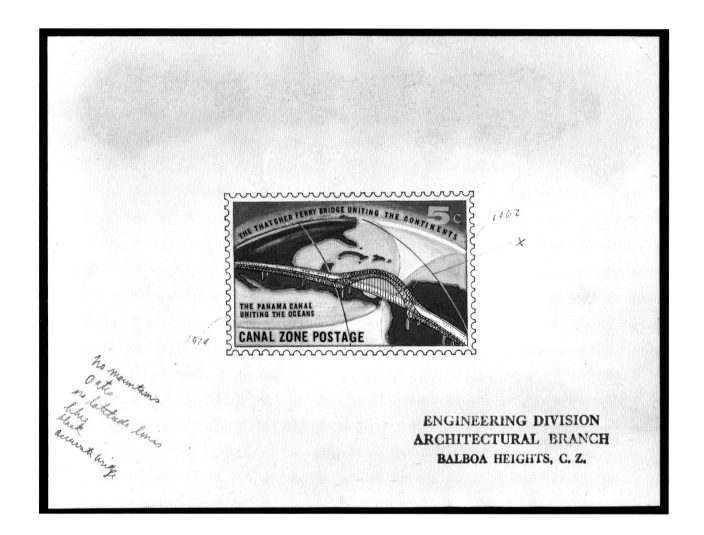

FIGURE 91
Rejected original art design for the
Thatcher Ferry Bridge stamp with
suggestions for changes.

—98—

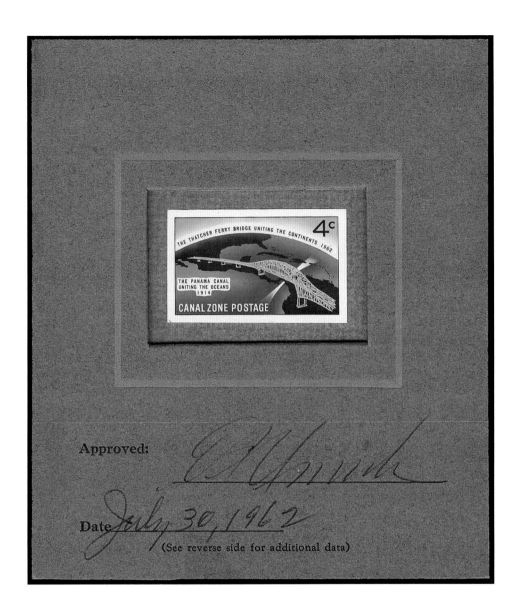

FIGURE 92

Model approved by Earl F. Unruh, director
of posts of the Canal Zone Postal Service,
for the final design of the Thatcher Ferry
Bridge stamp.

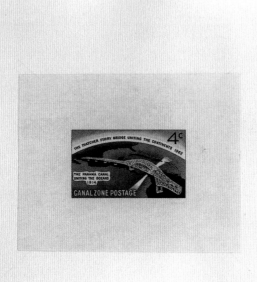

Approval of engraving and color hue:

Director of Posts

Original die proof approved August 17, 1962

FIGURE 93
Die proof of the Thatcher Ferry Bridge
stamp approved on 17 August 1962 by
Director Unruh.

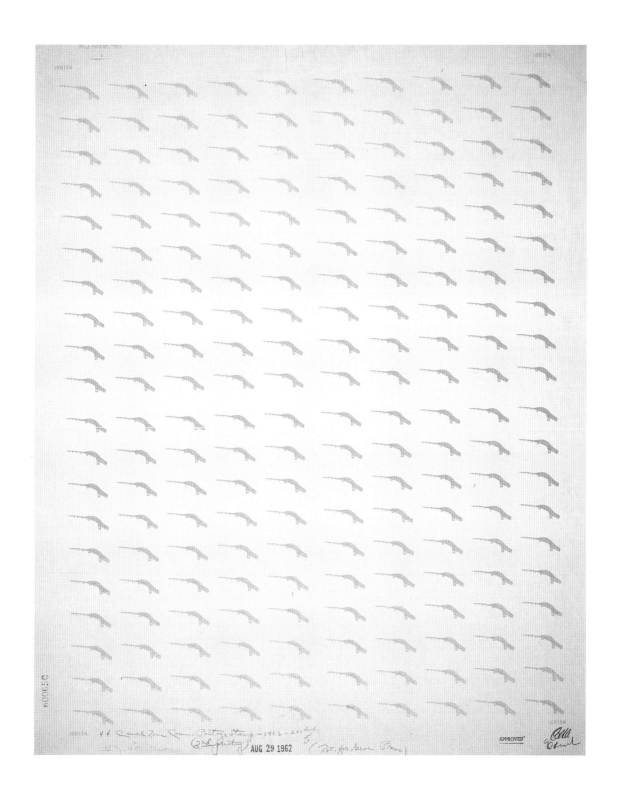

FIGURE 94

FIGURE 94
Approved certified plate proof for the plate
used to add the silver bridge over the map
of the Western Hemisphere.

Cable Address:
"HARRISCO" BOSTON

Telephone
KEnmore 6-8173
Area Code: 617

H. E. Harris & Co.

"THE WORLD'S LARGEST STAMP FIRM"

Postage Stamps and Philatelic Supplies

108 MASSACHUSETTS AVENUE
BOSTON 17, MASS.

October 17, 1962

Canal Zone Postal Service
Philatelic Agency
Balboa Heights, Canal Zone

Dear Sirs:

We have just received our order of the 4¢ Thatcher
Ferry Bridge stamp and we note that one of the sheets is without
the silver colored bridge printed thereon.

This is a most interesting deviation from normal and
we wonder if you may have more available that we could purchase.
If so, kindly let us know the quantity that are on hand without
the bridge shown and we will promptly send you a draft in pay-
ment.

We look forward to your reply and kindly use the en-
closed airmail special delivery stamped envelope.

Sincerely yours,

H. E. HARRIS & CO.

George Tarallo   +

Appraisal Department

G.Tarallo/jl

Enclosure

• Please mark your reply for the attention of the person signing this letter •

FIGURE 95

After discovering the missing bridge on a
pane, H. E. Harris & Company wrote to
the Canal Zone Postal Service to inquire
whether more were available for purchase.

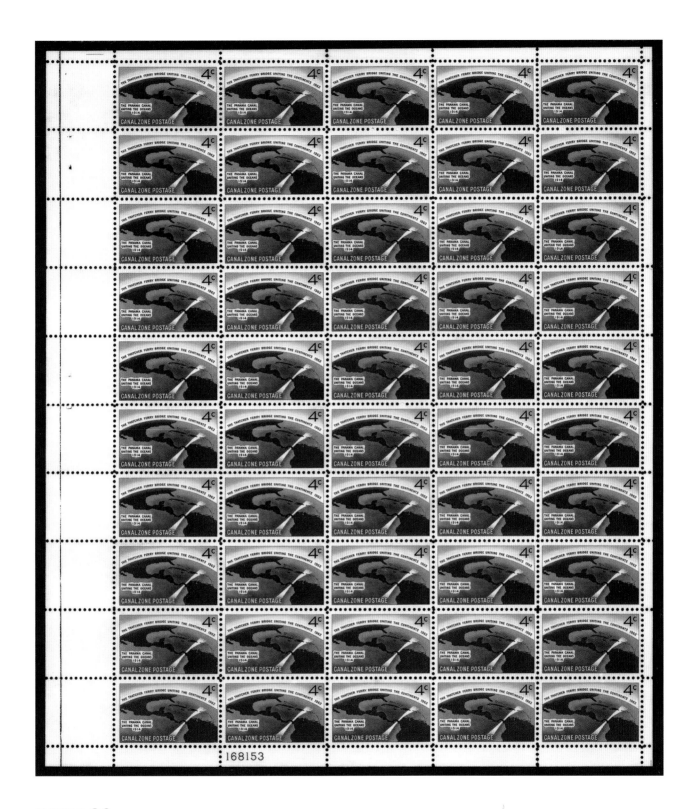

FIGURE 96

The Smithsonian Institution received the missing bridge lower left pane after
lamination in a 1966 transfer to its National Philatelic Collection.

15

THE INTERNATIONAL COLLECTIONS
Cheryl R. Ganz and Daniel A. Piazza

The National Philatelic Collection tells global stories, not just stories of the United States. International material comprises more than half the museum's holdings. Specialized collections range from Abu Dhabi to Zimbabwe. Many holdings tell the story of communications, history, culture, geography, and transport. In the vault are collections of Thurn and Taxis, the Napoleonic wars, zeppelin posts, autographs of famous personalities, topical selections ranging from maps to music, revenue stamps, and fakes and forgeries. These are represented through documents, stamps in all stages of production, stationery, and mail.

The Smithsonian's U.S. National Museum received two large and important collections of worldwide stamps early in the twentieth century. Donations from renowned philatelists began very early in the collection's existence. Between 1908 and 1915, David W. Cromwell, a prominent collector from New York City, donated a worldwide collection of approximately 22,000 stamps, most in unused condition. Three years later, the Post Office Department transferred the contents of its departmental museum to the Smithsonian, including nearly 200,000 Universal Postal Union (UPU) specimen stamps. During the late-nineteenth and early-twentieth centuries, the UPU in Switzerland distributed reference copies of recently issued stamps to postal administrations around the world. To prevent reuse, printers defaced the stamps, usually by overprinting the word "SPECI-MEN" (Figures 97 and 98).

These two collections formed the basis of the Smithsonian's first permanent philatelic exhibit, which was worldwide in scope. Its curator, Joseph Leavy, described its arrangement in the December 1914 issue of *Philatelic Gazette*: "Countries are displayed in alphabetical order, irrespective of geographical location. The headings throughout the collection give the date of issue, method of printing, where and by whom printed, watermark, and perforation, and if an issue is commemorative, a note is made of the event commemorated."

Curator Catherine Manning, who succeeded Leavy in 1922, sought to build as complete a general, worldwide collection as possible. Arthur Eugene Michel, a New York City advertising executive, bequeathed his virtually complete world-wide postal stationery collection to the Smithsonian in 1939. This outstanding collection of worldwide, government-issued postal stationery fills 143 volumes and comprises more than 40,000 objects. It represents fifty years of intensive and cumulative effort. At the time of its donation, it was 97 percent complete.

Manning's successors cultivated private donors and acquired highly specialized research collections of foreign stamps. Bernard Peyton, a chemical engineer and industrialist, donated several important collections of South American stamps. Chief among them was a collection of Peru formed by the noted philatelist Arthur Linz and purchased intact by Peyton. The finest portion of the collection is the volume dedicated to Peru's first stamps, the 1847 issue prepared for the Pacific Steam Navigation Company (Figure 99).

Leroy W. Christenson donated several collections of Asian stamps to the National Philatelic Collection, including eight volumes that once belonged to Alphonse Marie Tracey Woodward, the greatest student of Japan's first stamps. The albums, annotated in Woodward's handwriting, contain specialized collections of the 1-, 2-, and 4-sen issues of 1872–74 (Figure 100). Woodward's *Postage Stamps of Japan and Dependencies* (1928), based in part on the material in these volumes, is one of twentieth-century philately's rarest books. One hundred signed and numbered copies were printed on handmade vellum paper, bound in full calf leather, and adorned with tooled gold.

The Smithsonian National Postal Museum holds an exceptional group of internationally focused collections (Figures 101, 102, and 103). Many of these collections have been inventoried for finding guides, which are available online so researchers can study the scope, content, provenance, and list of materials in order to make plans to study the collection. Philatelic scholars are prolific writers, as evidenced by the many journals and publications in print and on-line. Many have studied the National Philatelic Collection to create definitive works in their specialized fields. Today, many more scholars are adding scientific methods of study to their research as new technology offers methods that do no harm to the philatelic objects but reveal underlying information.

FIGURE 97

China's 90¢ Curtiss Jenny airplane over the Great Wall with Universal Postal Union SPECIMEN overprint, 1921.

FIGURE 98

In 1921, Jamaica planned to release this stamp to mark the abolition of slavery. It was canceled at the last moment, when falling sugar prices led to unrest among sugar and dock laborers, who were mostly black. Most of the few surviving copies are UPU specimens that had already been distributed to postal administrations.

FIGURE 99

Perkins Bacon & Company supplied the postmark and ink for this 1847 Pacific Steam
Navigation Company envelope from Peru. This example is the only one known from
Chorillos (Numeral 7).

Issue of July 20th 1872

1 SEN BLUE

Plate 3

Wove paper

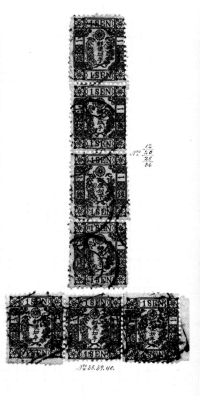

FIGURE 100

A. M. Tracey Woodward's plating study of the 1-sen blue, Japan, 1872, is part of his eight-volume research collection.

FIGURE 101

In 1845, the Grand Duchy of Finland was one of the first countries to issue prepaid envelopes. The 10-kopeck charge for domestic mailings was expensive, and relatively few were sold.

FIGURE 102

An 1855 registered cover from Senigallia to Rome bearing evidence of disinfection, probably during a cholera epidemic. Handstamped with the pontifical arms (crown and crossed keys) and the words *Netta Dentro e Fuori*, meaning "Cleaned inside and out."

FIGURE 103

The gem of the G. H. Kaestlin collection, this 1857 Tiflis City Post stamp is Russian philately's most desired item. Only five copies are known to exist. In 1937, Kaestlin acquired this one, which once belonged to Agathon Fabergé. Issued before the first imperial stamps for nationwide use, the Tiflis locals are similar to U.S. postmaster provisionals or Switzerland's cantonal issues.

16

INTERNATIONAL TREASURES
Daniel A. Piazza

The National Philatelic Collection holds millions of international stamps from more than 800 countries and stamp-issuing entities, including many that no longer exist. Philatelic treasures tell incredible stories and connect with important events in world history. Sometimes postal administrations and security printers unintentionally created scarce and rare stamps, stationery, or postal markings. Other treasures are the result of errors made during production, while a few represent "firsts" in the history of philately.

Not surprisingly, controversy often surrounds firsts, and postage stamps are no different. The National Philatelic Collection holds two contenders for the world's first prepaid postage stamp. Some experts believe that Greece issued an adhesive stamp for mail in 1831, which would make it, not Great Britain's Penny Black, the world's first stamp (Figure 104). Four covers are known bearing the stamps. However, all four of these covers date from after 1840, and the stamps do not seem to have been used for postage. One theory suggests that the proceeds, a sort of postal tax, went to a charity or public project. So the hand tips to the Penny Black, first issued in 1840.

The spread of prepaid, adhesive postage stamps around the globe can be charted through the National Philatelic Collection. Brazil's 1843 "Bulls-eyes" were the first national postage stamps issued in the Western Hemisphere (Figure 105). The bold designs feature the numerals 30, 60, or 90 reis within an oval—the origin of the nickname. Elaborate engraving behind the numerals made forgery difficult. The Sindh district issued Asia's first stamps in 1852, recalled two years later. The red stamp, embossed in fragile wax, is particularly scarce because over time the wax crumbled (Figure 106).

Of the myriad types of errors that can occur in postage stamp production, collectors covet the invert more than any other. The more arresting and striking the error—that is, the more improbable the subject becomes when turned on its head—the more famous and desirable it is. Most inverts exist in very small numbers, meaning only a few people can own them. The National Philatelic Collection holds some of the most famous international examples (Figures 107 and 108).

An 1895 stamp of the Belgian Congo features an image of Stanley Falls, a famous natural wonder. A single sheet of 100 stamps was printed with the waterfall inverted, complete with dozens of natives in upside-down canoes. About forty survive. In 1959, when Canada and the United States jointly issued a stamp to honor the 1959 opening of the St. Lawrence Seaway, a few sheets of the Canadian stamp were fed into the press upside down, inverting the image. The inverted stamp is one of only twenty-four that were actually used.

The National Philatelic Collection contains many examples of mail, often referred to as "covers," from early folded letters in the prestamp or stampless era to modern examples. Rarity can be attributed to who sent it or why, what adversity the cover encountered en route, or a postmark or auxiliary marking that is seldom found. Examples include Swedish "feather letters" from the mid-1700s to mid-1800s (Figure 109). A squiggly line represented Sweden's national symbol, three crowns for royal mail, and feathers directed that the letter should be delivered quickly. Another treasure sent through the mail was from a paddle steamer that carried mail around Trinidad. The captain of *Lady McLeod* issued stamps privately, of which only about forty have survived on cover (Figure 110).

Production and archival material offer glimpses into how stamp design and production have changed through the years. The 1854–55 Diadem Issue of New South Wales in Australia was printed in the colony using plates and pigments sent out by Perkins Bacon & Company, the London firm that also engraved the Penny Black (Figure 111). The Perkins Bacon craftsmen sent handwritten ink recipes explaining the pigments needed to obtain the desired colors. Trial printings of designs that were never issued are prized. The stamps intended to honor the millennium of Cairo's Al-Azhar Mosque are one example (Figure 112). Formerly in the collection of Egypt's King Farouk, the essays were seized and sold during the 1952 revolution that deposed him.

FIGURE 104

A 40-lepta Charity Tax single on cover,
Greece, 1848.

FIGURE 105
A 90-reis Bull's-eye single, Brazil, 1843.

FIGURE 106
A ½-anna Sindh Dak District Post single,
Sindh Dak, India, 1852.

FIGURE 107

A 10¢ River Scene on the Congo invert
error single, Congo Free State, 1895.

FIGURE 108

A 5¢ St. Lawrence Seaway invert error
single, Canada, 1959.

FIGURE 109

Feather letter, Sweden, ca. 1808.

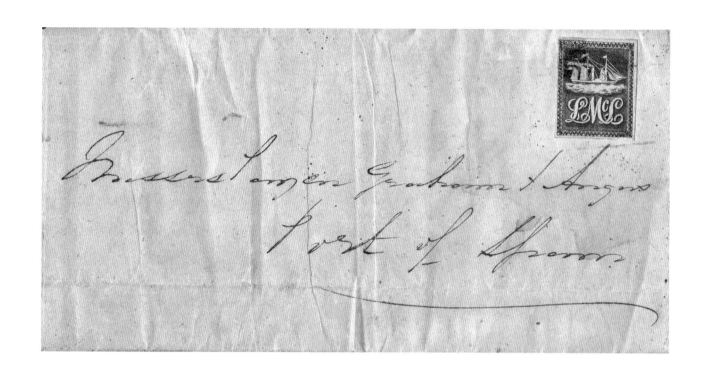

FIGURE 110
Lady McLeod cover, Trinidad, 1847.

FIGURE 111

Diadem Issue ink recipes and color proofs,
New South Wales, Australia, 1853.

FIGURE 112

A 20-millieme Millennium of Al-Azhar
Mosque essay, Egypt, 1942.

17

THE WILLIAM H. GROSS STAMP GALLERY
Cheryl R. Ganz

The William H. Gross Stamp Gallery opened on 22 September 2013 to showcase the world's largest museum postage stamp collection in the world's largest postage stamp gallery. First and foremost, the gallery spaces focus on the visitor experience, featuring exhibits with compelling stories that connect to visitors' lives. Creating the gallery was a ten-year journey.

In 2004, Curator of Philately W. Wilson Hulme II discussed replacing the existing permanent stamp gallery exhibits, especially to upgrade the quality of the objects on display. He and members of the Council of Philatelists selected representative examples for a new exhibit of U.S. stamps. Curator Cheryl R. Ganz joined the project in 2005, when redesigning the existing gallery space, a room with pullout frames on the lower level, was the goal. Of great concern, the space was too small and expansion impossible. Tragedy struck when Hulme died unexpectedly in January 2007.

Ganz soon facilitated a brainstorming session with museum staff to conceptualize an ideal or "dream museum" for a Philatelic Center of Excellence. When Hubert N. "Jay" Hoffmann III, a member of the Council of Philatelists, toured the museum and building, he told museum director Allen Kane that there was only one true option: expand to the street level. As a result, Ganz coordinated the "William H. Gross Stamp Gallery Expansion Project Plan" with input from over 100 stakeholders for a move of the philately gallery to the upper level, then occupied by a restaurant (Figure 113).

The stars aligned. The United States Postal Service agreed to a long-term lease of the space to the museum, signed in November 2007. Following a preliminary design study, William H. Gross offered to be the principal donor, and the architecture and design teams began work in March 2010.

An interview with museum director Allen Kane reveals some of the project's challenges.

Ganz: You have often said that this stamp gallery never should have happened. Why is that?

Kane: I figured out what had to happen to make it work, and it just didn't seem possible to get through all the politics and all the different major tasks—to get the space we needed, to get the Board of Regents of the Smithsonian to approve it, and to get the historical commissions to approve what we wanted to do. It seemed mind boggling, so I didn't think it had much of a chance.

Ganz: What was one of the greatest accomplishments for you in this project?

Kane: I really struggled very hard to stay out of a lot of the things that were happening and not micromanage. There were a lot of moving targets in this project and a lot of great people. The collaboration of the museum exhibition team and staff with Smithsonian Institution staff and multiple units, the museum's three advisory boards, volunteers, donors, and contractors, including Cho Benn Holback + Associates, architecture; Gallagher & Associates, design; Design and Production, fabrication; and Richard Lewis Media Group, films and interactives, ensured success (Figure 114).

Ganz: How did the Council of Philatelists, an advisory board, contribute to that success?

Kane: The Council of Philatelists helped us with feedback on gallery concepts, publicity, and networking to raise the millions of dollars needed for such a major undertaking. I actually can't think of a more valuable group (Figure 115).

Ganz: What is important for the collection and museum in the future?

Kane: We need to involve more people in philately. Stamps are pure education, and so the new gallery includes an education learning loft. We must incorporate technology in exhibits and steadily improve the museum's award-winning website to get our message out (Figures 116–119).

Ganz: What was your proudest moment?

Kane: When we cut the ribbon and opened the gallery.

FIGURE 113
Memorandum of Understanding signed
by (left to right) Patrick R. Donahoe,
Postmaster General, United States Postal
Service, and Richard Kurin, Under
Secretary for History, Art, and Culture,
Smithsonian Institution, in January 2007.

FIGURE 114

The June 2012 William H. Gross Stamp Gallery groundbreaking ceremony attendees included representatives from the Smithsonian Institution, National Postal Museum's Council of Philatelists, United States Postal Service, and Clark Construction. Front row (left to right): Karen Bertha, Glen Hopkins, Daniel A. Piazza, Stephen Kearney, Charles Shreve, Donald Sundman, Albert Horvath, Allen Kane, Richard Kurin, Cheryl R. Ganz, Wade E. Saadi. Back row (some partial view): Bruce Kendall, Vince King, Gordon E. Eubanks Jr., Trish Kaufmann, Robert G. Rose, Roger Brody, Omar Rodriguez, Steven J. Rod, Janet Klug, David Straight, May Day Taylor, Robert Odenweller, MaryAnn Bowman, Michael E. Aldrich, Sonny Hagendorf, James Kloetzel, David Herendeen, Elizabeth M. Hisey, John M. Hotchner. Back row (partial or hidden view): Ian C. Gibson-Smith, Thomas Lera, Marvin R. Murray Jr.

FIGURE 115
Allen Kane, director; Glen Hopkins, design
and construction manager; and Cheryl R.
Ganz, lead curator, place a time capsule
containing mementos of the museum,
philately, and 2013 behind the walls of the
Gems of American Philately gallery.

FIGURE 116

Cutting the ribbon to open the William H.
Gross Stamp Gallery are (left to right)
Cheryl R. Ganz, chief curator of philately;
Donald Sundman, chair, Council of
Philatelists; G. Wayne Clough, secretary,
Smithsonian Institution; William H. Gross,
lead donor; Patrick R. Donahoe, postmaster
general, United States Postal Service; Allen
Kane, director, National Postal Museum;
and Charles Shreve, co-chair, External
Affairs Committee.

FIGURE 117

Visitors approach the Gems of American Philately gallery through a dazzling arcade of oversized stamps and video monitors. The gems have captured stories from important moments in U.S. history.

FIGURE 118

Interactives offer creative possibilities
with every modern American stamp. The
Stamps Around the Globe gallery features
stamps and mail from every country that
has issued stamps.

FIGURE 119
The National Stamp Salon showcases
specialized U.S. collections, including
artifacts, revenue stamps, Kingdom of
Hawaii stamps, Canal Zone philately, and
United States Postal Service's Postmaster
General's Collection stamp artwork.

18

WINDOWS INTO AMERICA
Cheryl R. Ganz

No longer simply functional, the exterior windows of the Smithsonian National Postal Museum now tell a sweeping story, and they are called "Windows into America." Transformed by stamp art that visually narrates the museum's two themes, "Every Stamp Tells a Story" and "America's History is in the Mail," the windows excite, educate, and beckon. Critically selected from the National Philatelic Collection to complement architect Daniel Burnham's Beaux-Arts design for the capital's main post office, the fifty-four images of stamp art provide a stunning backdrop for the world's largest stamp gallery (Figure 120).

While planning the William H. Gross Stamp Gallery, architects and designers faced serious problems—protecting the gallery's fragile paper objects from sunlight's damaging rays and temperature fluctuations. The architects, designers, exhibition team, and Council of Philatelists brainstormed, finally selecting a solution that resolved all issues while preserving the windows' architectural integrity. By using a custom, removable glass system with laminated layers, including translucent graphics, the windows design reduced light levels, managed temperature shifts, and added security while allowing subtle sunlight into the gallery. In addition, the windows became an extraordinary design element unto themselves (Figure 121).

The pleasure of selecting stamps whose images would revolutionize the huge windows fell to the philatelic curators, Cheryl R. Ganz and Daniel A. Piazza. First and foremost, the two wanted stamps with images representing both significant historical events and the history of postal operations. Their first selection included 200 images from the approximately 4,000 stamps issued by the U.S. Post Office since 1847. From that group, designers chose fifty-four stamps that illustrate a broad swath of America's story and accommodate the design team's vision—iconic images that depict Americana, historical turning points, culture and arts, people and diversity, founding fathers, and representatives of post office operations and stamp collecting.

Designer Maria Felenyuk weighed the rhythm and scale of the stamps relative to the interior exhibitions. She created topical groups that created subtle color shifts across the gallery. In addition, designers evaluated upper and lower windows to craft a continuity of approach, balancing the architectural rhythm as viewed from the building exterior.

Windows into America's nighttime illumination gives life to this great public building in ways that even Daniel Burnham could not have imagined. The exquisite stamp art celebrates the building's original use as the main post office of Washington, D.C., as well as its current use as the Smithsonian National Postal Museum. Sponsored by Mark Porterfield, the windows fascinate passersby with their iconic images, they educate, and they invite everyone to learn more by stepping inside the monumental structure and the William H. Gross Stamp Gallery.

FIGURE 120
Smithsonian National Postal Museum with
Windows into America lit.

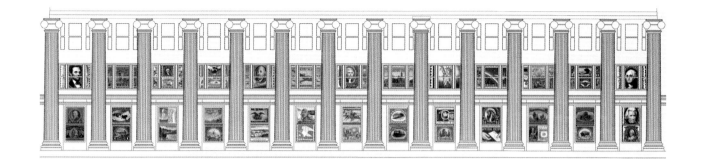

FIGURE 121

Windows into America. Bay one: 15¢ Abraham Lincoln, 1866; 10¢ Booker T. Washington, 1940; $5 Christopher Columbus, 1893. Bay two: 10¢ Special Delivery Messenger on Motorcycle, 1922; $1 Western Cattle in Storm, 1898; $1 Lincoln Memorial, 1923. Bay three: 3¢ Byrd Antarctic Expedition II, 1933; $2 James Madison, 1903; 3¢ Steam Locomotive, 1869; 5¢ Old Faithful, 1934; 32¢ Empire State Building, 1998; 6¢ Crater Lake, 1934. Bay four: 5¢ International Cooperation Year, 1965; 4¢ Arctic Explorations, 1959; 25¢ Transpacific *China Clipper*, 1935; $2 U.S. Capitol, 1923. Bay five: 3¢ Postage Stamp Centenary, 1947; 6¢ Eagle Holding Shield, Olive Branch, and Arrows, 1938; 4¢ First Automated Post Office, 1960. Bay six: 5¢ DC-4 Skymaster, 1946; 29¢ National Postal Museum, 1993; A Rate (15¢) Eagle, 1978. Bay seven: 5¢ Thomas Jefferson, 1861; 2¢ Thomas Edison's First Electric Lamp, 1929; 2¢ Olympic Winter Games Skier, 1932; 3¢ Pony Express, 1940; 3¢ Betsy Ross, 1952. Bay eight: 3¢ Smithsonian Institution, 1946; 24¢ Curtiss Jenny Invert, 1918; 2¢ *Empire State Express* Train, 1901. Bay nine: 8¢ Statue of Liberty, 1954; 4¢ St. Lawrence Seaway, 1959; $5 Head of the *Statue of Freedom*, 1923. Bay ten: $2.40 Moon Landing, 1989; 4¢ Project Mercury *Friendship 7* Capsule, 1962; 14¢ Chief Hollow Horn Bear, 1923; 20¢ Hand to Hand Special Delivery, 1954. Bay eleven: 34¢ Honoring Veterans, 2001; 5¢ Four Freedoms, 1946; 16¢ Great Seal of the United States, 1934; 20¢ Medal of Honor, 1983; 5¢ Pilgrim Tercentenary *Signing of the Compact*, 1920; 4¢ Fleet of Columbus Error of Color, 1893; 5¢ Jamestown Exposition *Pocahontas*, 1907; 13¢ "H. I." Hawaiian Missionary, 1852. Bay twelve: 10¢ Charles Lindbergh's Plane *Spirit of St. Louis*, 1927; 10¢ Samuel L. Clemens (Mark Twain), 1940; 16¢ Air Service Emblem, 1923; 10¢ Jane Addams, 1940; 10¢ *Hardships of Emigration*, 1898; 30¢ American Buffalo, 1923. Bay thirteen: 12¢ George Washington, 1861; 2¢ Andrew Jackson, 1875; 8¢ Martha Washington, 1902.

RESOURCES

Smithsonian National Postal Museum curators and staff have written many articles about objects or collections within the National Philatelic Collection. Their work has appeared in numerous publications, including *American Philatelist*, *Collectors Club Philatelist*, *Confederate Philatelist*, *Linn's Stamp News*, *London Philatelist*, *Philatelic Gazette*, *Smithsonian*, and *U.S. Specialist*. The museum website, http://www.postalmuseum.si.edu, includes exhibition stories and images, finding guides, Object of the Month stories, and blog posts. The museum online collection database site, http://www.arago.si.edu, includes individual object narratives as well as Featured Collection stories.

Collins, Herbert R. "The National Philatelic Collection: A Century of Collecting, 1886–1986." *American Philatelist* 100, no. 5 (1986): 430–40.

Ganz, Cheryl R. *Pacific Exchange: China & U.S. Mail*. Washington, D.C.: Smithsonian National Postal Museum, 2014.

Ganz, Cheryl R., and Daniel A. Piazza. *Delivering Hope: FDR & Stamps of the Great Depression*. Washington, D.C.: Smithsonian National Postal Museum, 2009.

———. *Fire & Ice: Hindenburg and Titanic*. Washington, D.C.: Smithsonian National Postal Museum, 2012.

John, Richard R. *Spreading the News: The American Postal System from Franklin to Morse*. Cambridge, Mass.: Harvard University Press, 1995.

Klug, Janet. *Guide to Stamp Collecting*. New York: Collins, 2008.

Lera, Thomas, and Leon Finik. *The G. H. Kaestlin Collection of Imperial Russian and Zemstov Stamps*. Washington, D.C.: Smithsonian Institution Scholarly Press, 2012.

Piazza, Daniel A. "Collecting History: 125 Years of the National Philatelic Collection." Smithsonian National Postal Museum. Last modified March 13, 2014 http://www.postalmuseum.si.edu/collectinghistory/index.html.

Rivinus, E[dward] F. "Spencer Fullerton Baird: The Collector of Collectors." *American Philatelist* 103, no. 11 (1989): 1061–5.

Scheele, Carl H. "A New Home for the Smithsonian's Philatelic and Postal History Collections." In *The Congress Book 1964*, pp. 11–14. Washington, D.C.: American Philatelic Congress, 1964.

Smithsonian National Postal Museum. "Finding Guides." Last modified April 16, 2014 http://www.postalmuseum.si.edu/findingguides/index.html.

Trepel, Scott R. *Rarity Revealed: The Benjamin K. Miller Collection*. With Ken Lawrence. Washington, D.C.: Smithsonian National Postal Museum, 2006.

CONTRIBUTORS

Richard Bates is a guest curator and research associate at the Smithsonian National Postal Museum. He holds a PhD in chemistry and is professor emeritus at Georgetown University. He is currently editor of *The Canal Zone Philatelist*, published by the Canal Zone Study Group, of which he served as president or vice-president for fourteen years. His area of expertise is Canal Zone philately, particularly overprinted U.S. issues.

Cheryl R. Ganz, curator emerita, was chief curator of philately of the Smithsonian National Postal Museum and lead curator of the William H. Gross Stamp Gallery. Ganz earned her PhD in history from the University of Illinois at Chicago. Her book *The 1933 Chicago World's Fair: A Century of Progress* earned the Smithsonian Secretary's Research Prize in 2011. Her areas of expertise are zeppelin posts, U.S. philately, Great Depression, and world's fairs.

Lynn Heidelbaugh is a curator in the History Department of the Smithsonian National Postal Museum. She curated the permanent exhibit *Mail Call: America's Military Mail*. Her areas of expertise are military postal history, U.S. postal operations, business history, tourism, and tourist industry history.

Richard R. John is professor at the Columbia Journalism School and a core member of Columbia's history faculty, where he teaches in Columbia's PhD program in communications. He is the author of *Spreading the News: The American Postal System from Franklin to Morse* and editor of *The American Postal Network, 1792–1914*, a four-volume collection of original source documents on topics in American postal history.

Ronald E. Lesher is a guest curator at the Smithsonian National Postal Museum. Lesher earned his EdD in research and measurement from Lehigh University. His areas of expertise are the federal and state revenue stamps of the United States, especially those used for the taxation of beer, wine, and liquor.

Daniel A. Piazza is a curator of philately of the Smithsonian National Postal Museum and served as lead curator for the international exhibits in the William H. Gross Stamp Gallery. He is president of NAPEX, National Philatelic Exhibitions of Washington, D.C., one of the leading stamp shows in America. His areas of expertise are early U.S. history plus U.S., Italian, and Vatican philately.

Nancy A. Pope is head curator in the History Department at the Smithsonian National Postal Museum. In 1993 she curated the opening exhibits for the museum. Most recently she curated *Systems at Work*, which delves into the inside world of U.S. postal operations. Her areas of expertise are the history of U.S. postal operations and transportation and technology history.

M. T. Sheahan is a script writer and editor for Smithsonian National Postal Museum exhibits and its website. She earned her PhD in history from Northern Illinois University. Working with philatelic curators Ganz and Piazza, she has worked on *Delivering Hope: FDR & Stamps of the Great Depression*, *Collecting History: 125 Years of the National Philatelic Collection*, *Fire & Ice: Hindenburg and Titanic*, *Favorite Finds*, and the *National Stamp Collection*.

INDEX

Numbers in *italic* indicate pages with illustrations